BRAINWASHING

A Synthesis of The Russian Textbook on Psychopolitics

Original Concept by Charles Stickley, New York, 1955
Original text with footnotes for the 21st Century
© Copyright 2005 - David J. Todeschini - all rights reserved

ISBN 1-4116-1822-X

Web site: www.Net4TruthUSA.com
Bookstore: www.LuLu.com/Net4TruthUSA

Net4TruthUSA.com
WebPastor David Todeschini

DISCLAIMER

The author of this book has studied Dianetics and Scientology, and some references appear in the text. The content of this book expresses the views and opinions of the author, and are in no way connected or affiliated with the Dianetics Foundation, or the Church of Scientology.

INTRODUCTION
By: WebPastor David Todeschini

This book was sent by the original author, Charles Stickley,[1] to the Church of Scientology[2] and to the Church of Christ, Scientist[3] in 1955. Included in this rendition, is the original manuscript largely word-for-word,[4] plus my running footnote commentary, and supplementary articles and dissertations to bring the original up-to date with modern developments and technologies. This book is a "synthesis" – in other words, it is not an "official" Russian document. However, it does, in its original text, accurately describe many of the methodologies in practice at the time it was written (circa 1955), and appears to have incorporated into it, the obverse of Dianetics technology called "Black Dianetics" by author and humanitarian L. Ron Hubbard.

This material in this manual has nothing whatsoever to do with Dianetics, Scientology, or Christian Science; it is the opposite of that technology, and those religions (respectively). The purpose of the original author in writing the original text is unknown; perhaps it was a warning to future generations who would read it, find its writings prophetic in retrospect, and become vigilant of the suppressive mentalities that seek to control every aspect of our lives. The original author is accurate in many respects, but could not have envisioned the 21st Century technology that could make the nightmare he and George Orwell envisioned, a stark reality.

This document came into my possession via a good friend in the Church of Scientology who understandably, wishes to remain anonymous. The friend was very close to the founder, L. Ron Hubbard, and is a very reliable source. Upon reading the copy he sent me, I thought that I would re-publish this manuscript, because although the USSR may now be defunct, the totalitarian mentality is still alive and thriving here in the United States.

The public needs to know these things, but in the hands of an idiot, this manual could prove dangerous to one's mental health. I take no responsibility for changes in attitude, or the mental conditions of my readers. You're old enough to decide for yourself – you've been warned!

My comments, when they fall within the original text will be   {bracketed}
Running corrections will appear in .... [square brackets]
All the footnotes are my own commentary on the original text.
Where the Bible is quoted, the 1611 King James Version is used, unless noted.

---

[1] This name could be an alias – there is no way to tell.
[2] When the synthesis was (allegedly) written in 1955, Scientology was a new religion in America.
[3] Church of Christ, Scientist - more commonly known as Christian Science.
[4] I have corrected gross spelling and grammatical errors when readability or clarity was adversely impacted.

For ease of readability, I, of necessity, took the liberty to correct gross grammatical errors,[5] and reformat some of the text, but it is presented here, largely verbatim. Please bear with excessive run-on sentences (so in the original), as the following text was transcribed from the original document that was sent to me. In order to preserve some of the original "flavor" of the document, I chose to leave some parts of it "as-is"; when this was done, I made a footnote: "- so in original".

The astute reader may find some of this material eerily prophetic. Some may argue that what is contained within these pages is "a conspiracy theory". I must enlighten those who do not believe in conspiracies, that there are conspiracy theories because there exists overwhelming evidence for the existence of conspiracies. According to the dictionary's definition of the word "conspiracy", conspiracies can consist of everything from a MAFIA drug cartel to two grammar school boys planning to pass quiz answers to each other.

Communism, or more precisely, what has been called "Champagne Socialism", is alive and well in the United States and the world today; of this there can be no doubt. The success of a conspiracy can be measured and determined by the unwillingness of the public to believe it when it is exposed. In this fashion, the "powers that be", or what the Bible in Romans chapter 8 calls "Principalities and Powers", and "Spiritual wickedness in high places", continue to lie, obfuscate, and spin the facts in order to manipulate the gullible public into believing anything they want us to believe. There are some of us who have learned to discern the lies. We need to listen to them.

{The original text of Charles Stickley's dissertation begins on the following page}

---

[5] Mr. Stickley, the original author, claimed to be a "professor", which is inconsistent with his poor grammar and sentence structure, which is largely preserved herein for effect.

EDITORIAL NOTE
By Charles Stickley (the original author)

This book is a synthesis of information gathered through observation, discussion, investigation, and experience over the last ten years {1945 to 1955}.[6]

I cannot entirely vouch for its authenticity. Disclosure of the sources, from which it is drawn, would undoubtedly lead to great difficulties for them. And in matters of this kind, the Soviet is not accustomed to the issuance of validations.

Having compiled this volume, I did not easily discover any method of distributing it, since my own facilities and finances are, as customary with professors, necessarily limited. Further, the placement of this volume in anyone's hands constituted to some degree, a considerable risk to myself until I realized that there actually were two American groups in the field of mental science who are entirely above suspicion, particularly since they were often mentioned in the actual text of this book as being antipathetic to this Soviet program. These two groups were the Christian Scientists and Church of Scientology. Christian Science is an American religion, intensely patriotic. Scientology (and its sub-study, Dianetics), also a religion, is the only entirely American development in the field of the human mind.[7]

Knowing from my information sources that the Church of Scientology and Christian Science and their people have experienced years of mauling and defamation at Communist hands, I am submitting to these organizations, this work.[8] I wish to express here, my appreciation for their bold resistance to Communism through the years.

---

[6] The reader must keep in mind that this text was written circa 1955.

[7] All of the "mental sciences" up to this point in time, originated in Germany or in Russia.

[8] A copy of the original treatise by Charles Stickley was sent to this author by a former Pastor of the Church of Scientology in a Midwestern state who wishes to remain anonymous.

I wish also to express my confidence in the future of the free nations of Earth. Although the Soviet has found a chink in the armor of individual liberty, it is certain that the Democratic processes can mend it. That only the individual himself can protest against assault and injury to him before law, joined with the fact that the insane have no rights before the law, has permitted in itself this deep ingress into our country's security. So long as this legal hole exists, there is then no law against driving anyone insane, even though this action deals as finally with a person as does murder. The existence today of highly efficient drugs such as LSD; one millionth of an ounce of which can create insanity, brings this legal loophole into focus. By enacting legislation permitting a friend or next-of-kin to bring charges in case of assault and by quickly placing all treatment of and institutions for the insane in the hands of ministers, taking it entirely out of the hands of European indoctrinated practitioners, the entire effort of Psychopolitics can be nullified at once.

If you care to check this subject of Psychopolitics against current occurrences in the American scene, you will discover the urgency of such measures.

Charles Stickley,
New York City, 1955

AN ADDRESS BY BERIA[9]

American students at Lenin University, I welcome your attendance at these classes on Psychopolitics.

Psychopolitics is an important if less-known division of Geo-politics. It is less known because it must necessarily deal with highly educated personnel; the very top strata of "mental healing". By Psychopolitics our chief goals are effectively carried forward. To produce a maximum of chaos in the culture of the enemy is our first and most important step. Our fruits are grown in chaos, distrust, economic depression, and scientific turmoil. At least a weary populace can seek peace only in our offered Communist State; at last only Communism can resolve the problems of the masses.

A Psychopolitician must work hard to produce the maximum chaos in the fields of "mental healing". He must recruit and use all the agencies and facilities of "mental healing". He must labor to increase the personnel and facilities of "mental healing" until at last, the entire field of mental science is entirely dominated by Communist principles and desires.

To achieve these goals, the Psychopolitician must crush every "home-grown" variety of mental healing in America. Actual teachings of Freud, James, Eddy, and others amongst your misguided peoples must be swept away. They must be discredited, defamed, arrested, stamped upon even by their own government, until there is no credibility in them, and only Communist-oriented "healing" remains. You must work until every teacher of psychology, unknowingly or knowingly teaches only Communist doctrine under the guise of "psychology". You must labor until every doctor and psychiatrist is either a Psychopolitician, or an unwitting assistant to our aims.

---

[9] "Beria" – It is unknown who this person is supposed to be – possibly an instructor in Psychopolitics.

You must labor until we have domain over the minds and bodies of every important person in your nation. You must achieve such disrepute for the state of insanity, and such authority over its pronouncement that not one Statesman so-labeled could again be given credence by his people. You must work until suicide arising from mental imbalance is common, and calls forth no general investigation or remark.

With the institutions for the insane, you have in your country, prisons[10] which can hold a million persons, and can hold them without civil rights or any hope of freedom. And upon these people can be practiced shock and surgery, so that never again will they draw a sane breath. You must make these treatments common and accepted, and you must sweep aside any treatment or any group of persons seeking to treat by effective means.

You must dominate as respected men the fields of psychiatry and psychology. You must dominate the hospitals and universities. You must carry forward the myth that only a European doctor is competent in the field of insanity and thus excuse amongst you the high incidence of foreign birth and training. If and when we seize Vienna you shall have then a common ground of meeting and can come and take your instructions as worshipers of Freud along with other psychiatrists.

Psychopolitics is a solemn charge. With that you can erase our enemies as insects. You can cripple the efficiency of leaders by striking insanity into their families through the use of drugs. You can wipe them away with testimony as to their insanity.[11]

---

[10] Prisons in the US are a hotbed of Psycho-quackery. Among the abuses are "treatments" on prisoners by totally unqualified persons. See report of the Department of Veterans Affairs Inspector General, case #2001-HL-0066, report #01-00290-22 dated October 31, 2001. Also see articles dealing with Prisoner Abuse on my web site at www.Net4TruthUSA.com/PrisonerAbuse.htm

[11] With Psychopolitics you can also efficiently and swiftly eliminate from the society any individual who poses a threat to a local effort to indoctrinate young people into our way of thinking. By drugging children in schools, we can make them easily susceptible, and win these already malleable minds over to our philosophy. By assuming the role of the

By our technologies you can even bring about insanity itself when they seem too resistive. You can change their loyalties by Psychopolitics. In a short time with a Psychopolitician, you can alter forever the loyalty of a soldier in our hands or Statesman or leader in his own country, or you can destroy his mind. However you labor under certain dangers. It may happen that remedies for our "treatments" may be discovered it may occur that a public-hue and cry may arise against "mental healing". It may thus occur that all mental healing might be placed in the hands of ministers and be taken out of the hands of our psychologists and psychiatrists. But the Capitalistic thirst for control, Capitalistic inhumanity and a general public terror of insanity can be brought to guard against these things. But should they occur, and should independent researchers actually discover means to undo Psychopolitical procedures, you must not rest, you must not eat or sleep and you must not stint one tiniest bit of available money to campaign against it, discredit it, strike it down and render it void. For by an effective means all our actions and researchers could be undone.

In a Capitalistic State you are aided on all sides of the corruption of the velocity of men and the times. You'll discover that everything will aid you in your campaign to season, control and you was all "mental healing" to spread our doctrine and rid us of our enemies within their own borders. Be used the courts, use the judges, use the Constitution of the country, use its medical societies and its laws to further our ends. Do not stint in your labor in this direction. And when you have succeeded you will discover that you can now effect your own legislation at will and you can, by careful organization of healing societies, by constant campaign about the terrors of society, by pretense as to your effectiveness make your Capitalist himself by his own appropriations, finance a large portion of the quiet Communist conquest of the nation.

---

protectorate of children, anyone can be eliminated by simply accusing them of harming those who are in our care and custody.

By Psychopolitics create chaos. Leave a nation leaderless. Kill our enemies, and bring to Earth Communism; the greatest peace man has ever known.

Thank you.

CHAPTER 1
THE HISTORY AND DEFINITION OF PSYCHOPOLITICS

Although punishment for its own sake may not be entirely without recompense, it is, nevertheless, true that the end and goal of all punishment is the indoctrination of the person being punished with an idea, whether that idea be one of restraint or obedience.

In that any ruler has, from time beyond memory, needed the obedience of his subjects in order to accomplish his ends, he has thus resorted to punishments. This is true of every tribe and State in the history of Man. Today, Russian culture has evoked more certain and definite methods of aligning and securing loyalties of persons and populaces, and of enforcing obedience upon them. This modern outgrowth of old practices is called Psychopolitics.

The stupidity and narrowness of nations not blessed with Russian reasoning has caused them to rely upon practices, which are today too ancient and outmoded for the rapid and heroic pace of our time. And in view of the tremendous advance of Russian Culture in the field of mental technologies, begun with the glorious work of Pavlov[12] and carried forward so ably by later Russians, it would be strange that an art and science would not evolve totally devoted to the aligning of loyalties and extracting the obedience of individuals and multitudes.

Thus we see that Psychopolitical procedures are a natural outgrowth of practices as old as Man; practices which our current in every group of men throughout the world. Thus in Psychopolitical procedures there is no ethical problem, since it is obvious and evident that Man is always coerced against his will to the greater good of the State, whether by economic gains or indoctrination into the wishes and desires of the State.

---

[12] Carried out experiments on dogs, concluding that if a dog can be made to salivate upon the sounding of a bell, a man could similarly be conditioned to respond to triggers in the environment.

Basically, Man is an animal.[13] He is an animal, which has been given a civilized veneer. Man is a collective animal, grouped together for his own protection before the threat of the environment. Those who group and control him must then have in their possession specialized techniques to direct the vagaries and energies of the animal Man, toward greater efficiency in the accomplishment of the goals of the State.

Psychopolitics, in one form or another, has long been used in Russia, but the subject is all but unknown outside the borders of our nation, save only where we have carefully transplanted our information and where it is used for the greater good of the nation.

The definition of Psychopolitics follows.

Psychopolitics is the art and science of asserting and maintaining dominion over the thoughts and loyalties of individuals, officers, bureaux,[14] and masses, and the effecting of the conquest of enemy nations through "mental healing". The subject of Psychopolitics breaks down into several categories, each naturally and logically proceeding from the last.

- Its first subject is the constitution and anatomy of man himself as a political organism.
- The next is an examination of man as an economic organism, as this might be controlled by his desires.
- The next is classification of State goals for the individual and masses.
- The next is an examination of loyalties.
- The next is the general subject of obedience.
- The next is the anatomy of the stimulus response mechanisms of Man.

---

[13] The idea that "man is an animal", is a basic tenet or doctrine of psychology. Scientology, as with every other religion on the planet, takes the obverse view that man has a soul that is immortal, and survives the death of his body. The truth is that man is more than just flesh, blood, and bone. Man is more, much more, then a mere physical existence.
[14] "Bureaux" - Bureau - (archaic form, so in original).

- The next is the subject of shock and endurance.
- The next is categories of experience.
- The next is the capitalizing and aligning of experience.
- The next is the use of drugs.
- The next is the use of implantation.
- The next is the general application of Psychopolitics within Russia.
- The next is the organization and use of counter-Psychopolitics.
- The next is the use of Psychopolitics in the conquest of foreign nations.
- The next is Psychopolitical organizations outside Russia, their composition, and activity.
- The next is the creation of a slave philosophy in a hostile nation.
- The next is countering anti-Psychopolitical activities abroad, and the final one, the destiny of Psychopolitical rule in a scientific age.

To this might be added many subcategories, such as the nullification of modern weapons by Psychopolitical activity.

The strength and power of Psychopolitics cannot be overestimated, particularly when used in a nation decayed by pseudo intellectualism, where exploitation of the masses combines readily with Psychopolitical actions, and particularly when the greed of Capitalistic or Monarchial régimes has already brought about an overwhelming incidence of neurosis which can be employed as a groundwork for Psychopolitical action and a Psychopolitical corps.

It is part of your mission,[15] student, to prevent Psychopolitical activity to the detriment of the Russian State, just as it is your mission to carry forward in our nation and outside it, if you are so assigned, the missions and goals of Psychopolitics. No agent of Russia could be even remotely effective without a thorough grounding in Psychopolitics, and

---

[15] Although we can present no direct empirical evidence that an organized "Psychopolitical" personal team has Infiltrated our country as suggested by this text, no organization is required If such doctrines as are spelled out here, become the accepted beliefs of a nation. Since this book was written (1955), it is amazing how prophetic it is.

so you carry forward with you a Russian trust to use well what you are learning here.

CHAPTER 2
THE CONSTITUTION OF MAN AS A POLITICAL ORGANISM

Man is already a colonial aggregation of cells, and to consider him an individual would be an error.[16] Colonies of cells have gathered together as one organ or another of the body, and then these organs have, themselves, gathered together to form the whole. Thus we see that man himself is already a political organism, even if we do not consider a mass of men.

Sickness could be considered to be a disloyalty to the remaining organisms on the part of one organism. This disloyalty, becoming apparent, brings about a revolt of some part of the anatomy against the remaining whole, and we have, in effect, an internal revolution. The heart, becoming disaffected, falls away from close membership and service to the remainder of the organism, and we discover the entire body in all of its activities is disrupted because of the revolutionary activity of the heart. The heart is in revolt because it cannot or will not cooperate with the remainder of the body. If we permit the heart thus to revolt, the kidneys, taking the example of the heart, many in their turn rebel and cease to work for the good of the organism. This rebellion, multiplying to other organs and the glandular system, brings about the death of the "individual". We can see with ease that the revolt is death; that the revolt of any part of the organism results in death. Thus we see that there can be no compromise with rebellion. Like the "individual" man, the State is a collection of aggregations. The political entities within the State must, all of them, cooperate for the greater good of State lest the State itself fall asunder and die; for with the disaffection of any single distrust[17] we discover an example set for other districts, and we discover, at length, the entire State falling. This is the danger of revolution.

---

[16] When a man loses his individuality and his self-determinism, he becomes insane. A man is only insane as he is self-determined and is able to postulate a future.

[17] This sentence doesn't really make sense – so in original.

Look at Earth. We see here one entire organism. The organism of Earth is an individual organism. Earth has as its organs the various races and nations of men. Where one of these is permitted to remain disaffected, Earth itself is threatened with death.

The threatened rebellion of one country, no matter how small, against the total organism of Earth, would find Earth sick, and the cultural State of man to suffer in consequence. Thus, the putrescent illness of Capitalist States, spreading its pus and bacteria into the healthy[18] countries of the world would not do otherwise but bring about the death of Earth, unless these ill organisms are brought into loyalty and obedience and made to function for the greater good of the worldwide State.[19] The constitution of Man is so composed that the individual cannot function efficiently without the alignment of each and every part and organ of his anatomy. As the average individual is incapable in an unformed and uncultured State, as witness the Barbarians of the jungle,[20] so must he be trained into a coordination of his organic functions by exercise, education, and work toward specific goals.

We particularly and specifically note that the individual must be directed from without to accomplish his exercise, education, and work. He must be made to realize this, for only then can he be made to function efficiently in the role assigned to him.

The tenets of rugged individualism, personal determinism, self-will, imagination and personal creativeness are alike in the masses antipathetic to the good of the Greater State. These willful and unaligned forces are no more than illnesses which will bring about

---

[18] We only need to look at Russia, and the United States, and compare the "health" of our respective cultures to know that although the US is "sick", it is only as "sick" as it has accepted and embraced Communism in any form.

[19] The idea of "One World Government" and a "New World Order" of the Masons and Illuminati – DT

[20] Obviously a covertly racist comment.

disaffection, disunity, and at length the collapse of the group to which the individual is attached.

The Constitution of man lends itself easily and thoroughly to certain and positive regulation from without all of its functions, including those of thinkingness, obedience, and loyalties; and these things must be controlled if a greater State is to ensue.

While it may seem desirable to the surgeon to amputate one or another limb or organ in order to save the remainder, it must be pointed out that this expediency is not entirely possible of accomplishment where one considers entire nations. A body deprived of organs can be observed to be lessened in its effectiveness.[21]

The world deprived of the workers now enslaved by the insane and nonsensical idiocies of the Capitalists and Monarchs of Earth, would, if removed, create a certain disability in the worldwide State. Just as we see the victor forced to rehabilitate the population of a conquered country at the end of a war,[22] thus any effort to depopulate a disaffected portion of the world might have some consequence. However, let us consider the inroad of virus and bacteria hostile to the organism, and we see that unless we can conquer the germ, the organ, or organism, which it is attacking, will itself suffer. In any State we have certain Individuals who operate in the role of the virus and germ, and these, attacking the population or any group within the population, produced, by their self-willed greed, a sickness in the organ, which then gradually spreads to the whole.

The Constitution of Man as an individual body, or the constitutional a State or portions of the State as a political organism are analogous. It is the mission of Psychopolitics first to align the

---

[21] A body deprived of organs is a dead shell.

[22] It is not ironic that after having bombed Iraq into oblivion post 9-11-01, we (the US) seek to rebuild it? No one is "forcing" us to do it; we seek by doing so, to impose "Democracy" upon Iraq.

obedience and goals of the group, and then maintain their alignment by the eradication of the effectiveness of the persons and personalities, which might swerve the group toward disaffection. In our own nation, where things are better managed and where reason reigns above all else, it is not difficult to eradicate the self-willed bacteria, which might attack one of our political entities. But in the field of conquest, in nations less enlightened, where the Russian State does not yet have power, it is not as feasible to remove the entire self-willed individual. Psychopolitics makes it possible to remove that part of his personality which, in itself, is making havoc with the person's own constitution, as well as with the group with which the person is connected.

If the animal Man were permitted to continue undisturbed by counter-revolutionary propaganda, if you were left to work under the well-planned management of the State, we would discover little sickness amongst Man, and we would discover no sickness in the State. But where the individual is troubled by conflicting propaganda, where he is made the effect of revolutionary activities, where he is permitted to think thoughts critical to the State itself, where he is permitted to question those in whose natural charge he falls, we would discover his constitution to suffer. We would discover, from this disaffection, the additional disaffection of his heart and of other portions of his anatomy. So certain is this principle that when one finds a sick individual, could one search deeply enough, he would discover a misaligned loyalty and an interrupted obedience to that person's group unit.

There are those who foolishly have embarked upon some spiritual Alice in Wonderland voyage into what they call the "subconscious" or the "unconscious" mind, and who, under the guise of "psychotherapy" would seek to make well the disaffection of body organs, but it is to be noted that their results are singularly lacking Ii success.[23] There is no strength in such an approach. When hypnotism

---

[23] The author here is covertly alluding to the science of Dianetics, which is an empirically proven, efficable technology. This Statement on part of the original author, Charles Stickley, speaking for Communist philosophies, is obviously a lie.

was first invented in Russia it was observed that all that was necessary was to command the unresisting individual to be well in order, many times, to accomplish that fact. The limitation of hypnotism was that many subjects were not susceptible to its uses, and hypnotism has had to be improved upon in order to increase the suggestibility of individuals who would not otherwise be reached. Thus any nation has had the experience of growing well again, as a whole organism, when placing sufficient force in play against a disaffected group. Just as in hypnotism any organ can be commanded into greater loyalty and obedience, so can any political group be commanded into greater loyalty and obedience should sufficient force be employed. However, force often brings about destruction, and it is occasionally not feasible to use broad mass force to accomplish the ends in view. Thus it is necessary to align the individual against his desire not to conform.

Just as it is a recognized truth that Man must conform to his environment,[24] so it is a recognized truth, and will become more so as the years proceed, that even the body of Man can be commanded into health.[25] The constitution of man renders itself peculiarly adapted to realignment of loyalties. Where these loyalties are indigestible to the constitution of the individual itself, such as loyalties to the 'petite bourgeoisie', to the Capitalist, to anti-Russian ideas, we find the individual body peculiarly susceptible to sickness, and thus we can clearly understand the epidemics, illnesses, mass-neuroses, tumults and confusions of the United States and other Capitalist countries.[26]
Here we find the worker improperly and incorrectly loyal, and thus we find the worker ill. To save him and establish him correctly and properly upon his goal toward a greater State, it is an overpowering

---

[24] It is a proven fact that a man who conforms to his environment, is not a well man. A man is at the pinnacle of his mental health, when he can cause the environment to conform to him; to serve his desires – conforming the environment to himself.

[25] It is true that the mind affects the body; this is the basis for the study of Dianetics.

[26] It is interesting how the author here, mixes a bit of truth - about the body's alignment with itself for health - with the lie that man must conform to the environment to be healthy. There is no truth to the latter Statement, as anywhere in the world where man fails to subdue his environment, he is on the very precipice of death, both physically and spiritually.

necessity to make it possible for him to grant his loyalties in a correct direction. In that his loyalties are swerved and his obedience cravenly demanded by persons antipathetic to his general good, and in that these persons are few, even in a Capitalist nation, the goal and direction of Psychopolitics is clearly understood.

To benefit the worker in such a plight, it is necessary to eradicate, by general propaganda, by other means, and by his own cooperation and self-willedness,[27] the perverted leaders. It is necessary, as well, to indoctrinate the educated strata into the tenets and principles of cooperation with the ideas and ideals of the Communist State.

The technologies of Psychopolitics are directed to this end.

---

[27] "Self-Willedness" - No such word in the English language - so in original.

CHAPTER 3
MAN AS AN ECONOMIC ORGANISM

Man is subject to certain desires and needs which are as natural to his beingness[28] as they are to that of any other animal.[29] Man, however, has the peculiarity of exaggerating some of these beyond the bounds of reason. This is obvious through the growth of leisure classes, pseudo-intellectual groups, the "petite bourgeoisie", Capitalism, and other ills.

It has been said with truth, that one tenth of a man's life is concerned with politics and nine tenths with economics. Without food, the individual dies. Without clothing, he freezes, without houses and weapons; he is prey to the starving wolves. The acquisition of sufficient items to answer these necessities of food, clothing, and shelter, in reason, is the natural right of a member of an enlightened State. An excess of such items brings about unrest and disquiet. The presence of luxury items and materials, and the artificial creation and whetting of appetites, as in Capitalist advertising, are certain to accentuate the less desirable characteristics of Man.

The individual is an economic organism, in that he requires a certain amount of food, a certain amount of water, and must hold within himself a certain amount of heat in order to live. When he has more food than he can eat, more clothes than he needs to protect him, he then enters upon a certain idleness which dulls his wits and awareness, and makes him prey to difficulties which, in a less toxic State, he would have foreseen and avoided. Thus we have a glut being a menace to the individual.

It is no less difficult in a group. Where the group acquires too much, its awareness of its own fellows and of the environment is

---

[28] "Beingness" – The state of being or existence.
[29] Here we go again with the "Man is an animal" business!

accordingly reduced, and the effectiveness of the group in general is lost.

The maintaining of a balance between gluttony and need is the province of Economics proper, and is the fit subject and concern of the Communist State. Desire and want are a state of mind. Individuals can be educated into desiring and wanting more than they can ever possibly obtain, and such individuals are unhappy.[30] Most of the self-willed characteristics of the Capitalists come entirely from greed. He exploits the worker far beyond any necessity on his own part, as a Capitalist, to need. In a nation where economic balances are not controlled, the appetite of the individual is unduly whetted by enchanting and fanciful persuasions to desire, and a type of insanity ensues, where each individual is persuaded to possess more than he can use, and to possess it even at the expense of his fellows.

There is, in economic balances, the other side. Too great and too long [a] privation can bring about unhealthy desires which in themselves, accumulate if left alone more than the individual can use.[31] Poverty itself, as carefully cultivated in Capitalist States, can bring about an imbalance of acquisition. Just as a vacuum will pull into it masses, in a country where enforced privation upon the masses it permitted, and where desire is artificially whetted, need turns to greed, and one easily discovers in such States exploitation of the many for the benefit of the few. If one, by the technologies of Psychopolitics, were to dull this excessive greed in the few who possess it, the worker would be freed to seek a more natural balance. Here we have two extremes. Either one of them is an insanity. If we wish to create insanity we need only collect or deprive an individual at long length beyond the ability to withstand and we have a mental imbalance.

---

[30] It is true that people who have too much, and have too much Idle time on their hands, are prone to boredom, and in general, are not happy. The epidemic proportions of suicides in Hollywood, among the rich and famous attest to this fact. It is true as the Bible says, "...the love of money is the root of all evil". It is not the money itself; but the love of that money to the exclusion of all else, that causes this spiritual condition. Once contracted, this disease is intractable.
[31] Doesn't make sense – so in original.

A simple example of this is the alternation of too low with too high pressures in a chamber, an excellent Psychopolitical procedure. The rapidly varied pressure brings about a chaos wherein the individual will[32] cannot act and where other wills then, perforce, assume control.

Essentially, in an entire country one must remove the greedy by whatever means, and must then create and continue a semi-privation in the masses in order to command and utterly control the nation. A continuous hope for prosperity must be indoctrinated into the masses with many dreams and glut of commodity, and this hope must be counter-played against the actuality of privation and the continuous threat of loss of all economic factors in case of disloyalty to the State in order to suppress the individual wills of the masses.

In a nation under conquest such as America, our slow and stealthy approach need take advantage only of the cycles of booms and depressions inherent in Capitalistic nations in order to assert more and more strong control over individual wills. A boom is as advantageous as a depression for our ends, for during prosperity our propaganda lines must only continue to point up the wealth the period is delivering to the selected few to divorce their control of the State.

During the Depression one most only point out that it ensued as a result of the avarice of a few and the general political incompetence of the national leaders. The handling of economic propaganda is not properly the sphere of Psychopolitics, but the Psychopolitician must understand economic measures and Communist goals connected with them.

The masses must at last come to believe that the only the excessive taxation of the rich can relieve them of the "burdensome

---

[32] Should be reworded as "...the will of the individual cannot act" – so in original.

leisure class" and can thus be brought to accept such a thing as income tax, a Marxist principle smoothly slid into Capitalistic framework in {the year} 1909 in the United States. This even though the basic Law of United States forbade it and even though Communism at that time had been active only a few years in America. Such success as the Income Tax Law, had it been followed thoroughly could have brought the United States and not Russia into the world scene as the first Communist nation. But the virility and good sense of the Russian peoples won. It may not be that the United States will become entirely Communist until past the middle of the century but when it does it will be because of our superior understanding of economics and of Psychopolitics.

The Communist agent skilled in economics has as his task the suborning of tax agencies and their personnel to create the maximum disturbance and chaos and the passing of laws adapted to our purposes, and to him we must leave this task. The Psychopolitical operator plays a distinctly different role in this drama.

The rich, the skilled in finance, the well-informed in government are particular and individual targets for the Psychopolitician. His is the role of taking off the Board those individuals who would halt or corrupt Communist economic programmes. Thus every rich man, every Statesman, every person well informed and capable in government must have brought to his side as a trusted confidant, a Psychopolitical operator. The families of these persons are often deranged from idleness and glut, and this fact must be played upon; even created. The normal health and wildness of a rich man's son must be twisted and perverted and explained into neurosis and then, assisted by a timely administration of drugs or violence, turned into criminality or insanity. This brings at once some one[33] in

---

[33] Should be "someone" – so in original.

"mental healing" into confidential contact with the family, and from this point on the very most must then be made of that contact.[34]

Communism could best succeed if, at the side of every rich or influential man there could be placed a Psychopolitical operator, an undoubted authority in the field of "mental healing" who could then, by his advice or guided opinions, or through the medium of a wife or daughter, direct the optimum policy to embroil or upset the economic policies of the country and, when the time comes to do away forever with the rich or influential man, to administer the proper drug or treatment to bring about his complete demise in an institution as a patient or his death by suicide.

Planted beside the country's powerful persons the Psychopolitical operator can also guide other policies to the betterment of our battle.

The Capitalist does not know the definition of war. He thinks of war as an attack with force performed by soldiers and machines. He does not know that a more effective if somewhat longer war and before it with bread or, in our case, with drugs and the wisdom of our art. The Capitalist has never won a war in truth. The Psychopolitician is having little trouble winning this one.

---

[34] This has largely been accomplished by the infiltration of psychiatry and psychology into our public schools, with the attendant rise of mental illness among children, along with increased rates of teen suicide, which is directly attributed to the doctrines of evolutionists, and a meddling of social workers into the private lives of the American family.

CHAPTER 4
STATE GOALS FOR THE INDIVIDUAL AND MASSES

Just as we would discover an Individual to be ill, whose organs, each one, had a different goal for the rest, so we discover the individuals and the State to be ill where goals are not rigorously codified and enforced. There are those who, in less enlightened times, gave Man to believe that goals should be personally sought and held, and that, indeed, Man's entire impulse toward higher things stemmed from Freedom. We must remember that the same people who embraced this philosophy also continued in Man the myth of spiritual existence.[35]

All goals proceed from duress[36]. Life is a continuous escape.[37] Without force and threat there can be no striving. Without pain there can be no desire to escape from pain.[38] Without the threat of punishment there can be no gain.[39] Without duress and command there can be no alignment of bodily functions. Without rigorous and forthright control, there can be no accomplished goals for the State.

Goals of the State should be formulated by the State for the obedience and concurrence of the individuals within that State. A State without goals so formulated is a sick State. A State without the power and forthright wish to enforce its goals is a sick State.

When an order is issued by the Communist State, and is not obeyed, a sickness will be discovered to ensue. Where obedience fails, the masses suffer.[40]

---

[35] "Myth", indeed! One can go to Hell without believing in it.

[36] The basic motivator of Man is to survive. In Dianetics and Scientology, this is called "The First Dynamic".

[37] In Russia, I imagine that this Statement is empirical truth.

[38] Without pleasure, there can be no desire to pursue happiness (or pleasure).

[39] Where punishment is present, a person tends to assert that he's right, even though he's wrong.

[40] Where compulsion exists, and self-determinism is not possible, the nation sinks to apathy, no creativity exists, and the incentive to innovate and improve life's conditions disappears.

State goals depend upon loyalty and obedience for their accomplishment. When one discovers a State goal to be interpreted, one discovers inevitably that there has been an interposition of self-willedness[41] greed, of idleness, or of rugged individualism and self-centered initiative. The interruption of a State goal will be discovered as having been interrupted by a person whose disloyalty and disobedience is the direct result of his own misalignment with life.

It is not always necessary to remove the individual. It is possible to remove his self-willed tendencies to the improvement of the goals and gains of the whole.

The technologies of Psychopolitics are graduated upon the scale, which starts somewhat above the removal of the individual himself, upward toward the removal only of those tendencies, which bring about his lack of cooperation.

It is not enough for the State to have goals. These goals, once put forward, depend for their completion upon the loyalty and obedience of the workers. These, engaged for the most part, in hard labors, have little time for idle speculation, which is good. But, above them, unfortunately, there must be foremen of one or another position, any one of whom might have sufficient idleness and lack of physical occupation to cause some disaffecting independence in his conduct and behavior.

Psychopolitics remedies this tendency toward disaffection when it exceeds the common persuasions of the immediate superiors of the person in question.

---

[41] "Self-willedness" - no such word in the English language (but we get the gist) - so in original.

CHAPTER 5
AN EXAMINATION OF LOYALTIES

If loyalty is so important in the economic and social structure it is necessary to examine it further as itself. In the field of Psychopolitics, loyalty means simply 'alignment'. It means, more fully, alignment with the goals of the Communist State. Disloyalty means entirely misalignment, and more broadly, misalignment with the goals of the Communist State.

When we consider that the goals of the Communist State are to the best possible benefit of the masses, we can see that disloyalty, as a term, can embrace Democratic alignment. Loyalty to persons not communistically indoctrinated would be quite plainly a misalignment.

The cure of disloyalty is entirely contained in the principles of alignment. All that it is necessary to do, where disloyalty is encountered, is to align the purposes of the individual toward the goals of Communism, and it will be discovered that a great many circumstances hitherto distasteful is his existence will cease to exist.

A heart or a kidney in rebellion against the remainder of the organism is being disloyal to the remainder of the organism. To cure that heart or kidney it is actually only necessary to bring its activities into alignment with the remainder of the body.

The technologies of Psychopolitics adequately demonstrate the workability of this. Mild shock of the electric variety can, and does, produce the re-cooperation of a rebellious body organ.[42] It is the shock and punishment of surgery, which in the main accomplishes the realignment of a disaffected portion of the body, rather than the surgery

---

[42] This was the mentality, in the days when we didn't know any better.

itself.[43] It is the bombardment of X-rays, rather than the therapeutic value of X-rays,[44] which causes some disaffected organ to once again turn its attention to the support of the general organism.

While it is not borne out that electric shock has any therapeutic value,[45] so far as making the individual more sane, it is adequately brought out that its punishment value will create in the patient a greater cooperative attitude.[46] Brain surgery has no statistical data to recommend beyond its removal of the individual personality from amongst the paths of organs, which were not permitted to cooperate.[47] These two Russian developments have never pretended to alter the State of sanity.[48] They are only effective and workable in introducing an adequate punishment mechanism to the personality to make its cease and desist from its courses and egotistical direction of the anatomy itself.

It is the violence of the electric shock and the surgery, which is useful in subduing the recalcitrant personality, which is all that stands in the road of the masses or the State. It is occasionally to be discovered that the removal of the preventing personality[49] by shock and surgery then permits the re-growth and reestablishment of organs, which have been rebelled against by that personality. In that a well-regulated State is composed of organisms, not personalities, the use of electric shock and brain surgery in Psychopolitics is clearly demonstrated.

---

[43] Please give me some of what this guy was smoking! - for "therapeutic" purposes only.

[44] The "therapeutic" value of x-rays is a new one on me!

[45] Shock of any kind, is NOT therapeutic in any way.

[46] Well, duuuhhh!- If you shocked me, I'd be plotting on how I could kill you – slowly.

[47] When you find out what this means, let me know – so in original.

[48] They don't have to pretend; insanity always follows "therapeutic" electroshock treatments. "Surgery" in the context here, is performed with dime store ice pick.

[49] I have no idea what a "preventing personality" is.

The changing of loyalty consists, in its primary step, of the eradication of existing loyalties. This can be done in one of two ways. First by demonstrating that previously existing loyalties have brought about perilous physical circumstances, such as imprisonment, lack of recognition, duress, or privation, and second by eradicating the personality itself.

The first is accomplished by a steady and continuous indoctrination of the individual in the belief that his previous loyalties have been granted to an unworthy source. One of the primary instances in this is creating circumstances, which apparently derive from the target of his loyalties, so as to rebuff the individual. As part of this there is the creation of a state of mind in the individual by actually placing him under duress, and then furnishing him with false evidence to demonstrate that the target of his previous loyalties is, itself, the course[50] of the duress. Another portion of this same method consists of defaming or degrading the individual whose loyalties are to be changed to the target of his loyalties, i.e., superiors or government, to such a degree that this target, at length, actually does hold the individual in disrepute, and so does rebuff him and serve to convince him that his loyalties have been misplaced. These are the milder methods, but have proven extremely effective. The greatest drawback in their practice is that they require time and concentration, the manufacture of false evidence, and the Psychopolitical operator's time.

In moments of expediency, of which there are many, the personality itself can be rearranged by shock, surgery, duress, privation and, in particular, that best of Psychopolitical techniques, implantation, with the technologies of neo-hypnotism. Such duress must have in its first part a defamation of the loyalties, and in its second, the implantation of new loyalties. A good and experienced Psychopolitical operator, working under the most favorable circumstances can, by the use of Psychopolitical technologies, alter the loyalties of an individual so deftly that his own companions will not suspect that they have

---

[50] Should read "cause of the duress" – so in original.

changed. This, however, requires considerably more finesse than is usually necessary to the situation. Mass neo-hypnotism[51] can accomplish more or less the same results when guided by an experienced Psychopolitical operator.

An end goal in such a procedure would be the alteration of the loyalties of entire nation in a short period of time by mass neo-hypnotism, a thing that has been effectively accomplished among the less-usable States of Russia.

It is adequately demonstrated that loyalty is entirely lacking in that mythical commodity known as "spiritual quality". Loyalty is entirely a thing of dependence, economic or mental, and can be changed by the crudest implementations. Observation of workers in their factories or fields demonstrates that they easily grant loyalty to a foreman or a woman, and then as easily abandon it and substitute another individual, revulsing,[52] at the same time, toward the person to whom loyalty was primarily granted.

The queasy insecurity of the masses in Capitalistic nations finds this more common than in an enlightened State such as Russia. In Capitalistic States, dependencies are so craven wants and privations are so exaggerated, that loyalty is entirely without ethical foundation[53] and exists only in the realm of dependency, duress, or demand.

It is fortunate that Communism so truly approaches an ideal state of mind, for this brings a certain easiness into any changing of loyalties, since all other philosophies extant and practiced on Earth

---

[51] Mass Neo-hypnotism is another word for some Madison Ave. marketing techniques.

[52] Should probably be "Revolting" - so in original.

[53] A person without ethics is driven by the baser instincts. A person addicted to a substance or drug, will do anything to obtain that substance to satisfy the craving.

today are degraded and debased, compared to Communism. It is then with a certain security that a Psychopolitical operator functions, for he knows that he can change the loyalty of an individual to a more ideal level by reason alone,[54] and only expediency makes it necessary to employ the various shifts of Psychopolitical technology. Any man who cannot be persuaded into Communist rationale is, of course, to be regarded as somewhat less than sane, and it is, therefore, completely justified to use the techniques of insanity upon the non-Communist.

In order to change loyalty it is necessary to establish first the existing loyalties of the individual. The task is made very simple in view of the fact that Capitalistic and Fascistic nations have no great security in the loyalty of their subjects.[55] And it may be found that the loyalties of the subjects, as we call any person against whom Psychopolitical technology is to be exerted, are already too faint to require eradication. It is generally only necessary to persuade with the rationale and overwhelming reasonability of Communism to have the person grant his loyalty to the Russian State. However, regulated only by the importance of the subject, no great amount of time should be expended upon the individual, but emotional duress, or electric shock, or brain surgery should be resorted to, should Communist propaganda fail. In a case of a very important person, it may be necessary to utilize the more delicate technologies of Psychopolitics so as to place the person himself, and his associates, in ignorance of the operation. In this case a simple implantation is used, with a maximum duress and command value.

Only the most skilled Psychopolitical operator should be employed on such a project, as in this case of the very important person, for bungling might disclose the tampering with his mental processes. It is much more highly recommended, if there is any doubt whatever about the success of an operation against an important person,

---

[54] Liberals and Communists alike, are adept at diverting a debate onto an irrelevant subject.
[55] Citizens in Capitalistic countries are free to choose; citizens in Police States traditionally seek to rebel against the suppressor nature of totalitarian governments.

to select out as a Psychopolitical target persons in his vicinity in whom he is emotionally involved. His wife or children normally furnish the best targets, and these can be operated against without restraint. In securing the loyalty of a very important person one must place at his side a constant pleader who enters a sexual or familial cord into the situation on the side of Communism. It may not be necessary to make a Communist out of the wife, or the children, or one of the children, but it might prove efficacious to do so. In most instances, however, this is not possible.

By the use of various drugs, it is, in this modern age, and well within the realm of Psychopolitical reality, entirely too easy to bring about a State of severe neurosis or insanity in the wife or children,[56] and thus pass them, with full consent of the important person and the government in which he exists, or the Bureau in which he is operating, into the hands of a Psychopolitical operator, who then in his own laboratory, without restraint or fear of investigation or censor can, with electric shock, surgery, sexual attack, drugs, or other useful means, degrade or entirely alter the personality of a family member, and create in that person a Psychopolitical slave subject who then, on command or signal, will perform outrageous actions, thus discrediting the important person, or will demand, on a more delicate level, that certain measures be taken by the important person, which measures are, of course, dictated by the Psychopolitical operator.

Usually when the Party has no real interest in the activities with decisions of the important person, but merely wishes to remove him from effective action, the attention of the Psychopolitical operator need not be so intense, and the person need only be passed into the hands of some unwitting mental practitioner, who taught as he is by

---

[56] Over 9,000,000 children in the United States are routinely given psychotropic drugs such as Ritalin™, Adderall™ ("speed"), or other dangerous medications in school, to treat nonexistent maladies such as "Attention Deficit Hyperactivity Disorder".

Psychopolitical operators, will bring about sufficient embarrassment. When the loyalty of an individual cannot be swerved, and where the opinion, weight, or effectiveness of the individual stands firmly in the road of Communist goals, it is usually best to occasion a mild neurosis into the person by any available means, and then, having carefully given him a history of mental imbalance, to see to it that he disposes of himself by suicide,[57] or to bring about his demise in such a way as to resemble suicide.[58] Psychopolitical operators have handled such situations skillfully tens of thousands of times within and without Russia.

It is the firm principle of Psychopolitics that the person to be destroyed must be involved at first or second hand in the stigma of insanity, and must have been placed in contact with Psychopolitical operators or persons trained by them, with a maximum amount of tumult and publicity. The stigma of insanity is properly placed at the door of such person's reputation and is held there firmly by bringing about irrational acts, either on his own part or in his vicinity. Such an activity can be classified as a partial destruction of alignment,[59] and if this destruction is carried forward to its furthest extent the misalignment on the subject of all loyalties can be considered to be complete, and alignment on new loyalties can be embarked upon safely. By bringing about insanity or suicide on the part of the wife of an important political personage, a sufficient misalignment has been instigated to change his attitude. And this carried forward firmly, or assisted by Psychopolitical implantation can begin the rebuilding of his loyalties, but now slanted in a more proper and fitting direction.

Another reason for the alignment of Psychopolitical activities with the mis-alignment of insanity is that insanity itself is a despised

---

[57] Perhaps this is what was done to Vincent Foster.

[58] The layman would be surprised to learn of how many of these "Covert Operations" are carried out daily, against the enemies of Communism around the world.

[59] This alignment is known in Scientology as the "A. R. C. triangle" - Affinity, Reality, Communication. Destroying anyone of these necessarily destroys the others also.

and disgraced state, and anything connected with it is lightly viewed.[60] Thus, a Psychopolitical operator, working in the vicinity of an insane person, can refute and disprove any accusations made against him by demonstrating that the family itself is tainted with mental imbalance.[61] This is surprisingly effective in Capitalistic countries where insanity is so thoroughly feared that no one would dream of investigating any circumstances in its vicinity[62]. Psychopolitical propaganda works constantly, and must work constantly to increase and build up this aura of mystery surrounding insanity, and must emphasize the horribleness[63] and hopelessness of insanity in order to excuse non-therapeutic actions taken against the insane.[64]

Particularly in Capitalistic countries, an insane person has no rights under law.[65] No person who is insane may hold property. No person who is insane may testify.[66] Thus we have an excellent road along which we can travel toward our certain goal and destiny.

Entirely by bringing about public conviction that the sanity of the person is in question, it is possible to discount and eradicate all of the goals and activities of that person. By demonstrating the insanity of a group, or even a government, it is possible, then, to cause its people to disavow it.

By magnifying the general human reaction to insanity, through keeping the subject of insanity itself forever before the public eye, and

---

[60] No one "in his/her right mind" would be caught dead on a psychiatrist's couch.

[61] With 347 different "mental disorders" defined in the Diagnostic and Statistical Manual (DSM-IV), the Psychopolitician does not suffer for a lack of "fitting" diagnoses, which can be tailored to anyone on the planet; these diagnoses are all a matter of opinion, anyway... and money and other motivations, can easily sway these "professional" opinions to effect the goals of the Communist Police State.

[62] It is commonly thought that insanity is contagious by association. This is known in Scientology as "The contamination of Aberration".

[63] "Horribleness" – no such word – so in original.

[64] Anything short of Dianetics or Scientology is a "non-therapeutic" intervention.

[65] Many States have liberal "Civil Commitment" laws, under which a person can be adjudicated as "insane", and held prisoner in a mental institution, where, if he isn't already insane, he will be driven to insanity.

[66] Who would believe the testimony of an insane person?

then, by utilizing this reaction by causing a revulsion on the part of a populace against its leader or leaders, it is possible to stop any government or movement.

It is important to know that the entire subject of loyalty is thus as easily handled as it is. One of the first and foremost missions of the Psychopolitician is to make an attack upon Communism and insanity synonymous. It should become the definition of insanity, of the paranoid variety, that, "A paranoid believes he is being attacked by Communists". Thus at once the support of the individual so attacking Communism will fall away and wither.

Instead of executing national leaders, suicide for them should be arranged under circumstances which question their demise.[67] In this way we can select out all opposition to the Communist extension into the social orders of the world, and render populaces who would oppose us leaderless, and bring about a state of chaos or misalignment into which we can thrust, with great simplicity, the clear and forceful doctrines of Communism.

The cleverness of our attack in this field of Psychopolitics is adequate to avoid the understanding of the layman and the usual stupid official, and by operating entirely under the banner of authority, with the oft-repeated statement that the principles of psychotherapy are too devious[68] for common understanding, an entire revolution can be effected without the suspicion of a populace until it is an accomplished fact.

As insanity is the maximum mis-alignment, it can be grasped to be the maximum weapon in {the} severance of loyalties to leaders and old social orders. Thus, it is of the utmost importance that Psychopolitical operatives infiltrate the healing arts of a nation marked

---

[67] Remember Vincent Foster?
[68] Too deviOUS or too deviANT?

for conquest, and bring from that quarter continuous pressure against the population and the government until at last the conquest is affected[69]. This is the subject and goal of Psychopolitics, itself.

In rearranging loyalties we must have a command of their values. In the animal the first loyalty is to himself.[70] This is destroyed by demonstrating [his] errors to him, showing him that he does not remember, cannot act or does not trust himself. [71]
The second loyalty is to his family unit, his parents and brothers and sisters,[72] This is destroyed by making a family unit economically non-dependent, by lessening the value of marriage,[73] by making an easiness of divorce and by raising the children wherever possible by the State.

The next loyalty is to his friends and local environment.[74] This is destroyed by lowering his trust and bringing about reportings upon him allegedly by his fellows or the town or village authorities. The next is to his State, and this, for the purposes of Communism, is the only loyalty, which should exist once the State is founded as a Communist State. To destroy loyalty to the State all manner of forbiddings[75] for youth must be put into effect so as to disenfranchise them as members of the Capitalist State and, by promises of a better lot under Communism, to gain their loyalty to a Communist movement.

Denying a Capitalist country easy access to courts, bringing about and supporting propaganda to destroy the home, creating continuous juvenile delinquency, forcing upon the State all manner of practices to divorce the child from it will in the end create the chaos necessary to {institute} Communism.

---

[69] "Affected" should be "effected" – so in original.
[70] In Scientology, the corollary is "The First Dynamic" (physical survival).
[71] A man is as sane as he is self-determined.
[72] In Scientology, the corollary is "The Second Dynamic" (family and procreation - the sex dynamic).
[73] Degrading the value of marriage, by sanctioning same-sex marriages is a Psychopolitical invention.
[74] In Scientology, the corollary is "The Third Dynamic" (groups - friends, race, Country, etc.).
[75] "Forbiddings" – no such word – probably means "the things that are forbidden" – so in original.

Under the saccharine guise of assistance to them, rigorous child labor laws are the best means to deny the child any right in the society.[76] By refusing to let him earn, by forcing him into unwanted dependence upon a grudging parent, by making certain in other channels that the parent is never in other than economic stress, the child can be driven in his teens into revolt[77]. Delinquency will ensue.

By making readily available drugs of various kinds, by giving the teenager alcohol, by praising his wildness, by stimulating him with sex literature[78] and advertising to him or her practices as taught at the Sexpol,[79] the Psychopolitical operator can create the necessary attitude of chaos, idleness, and worthlessness into which can then be cast the solution which will give the teenager complete freedom everywhere – Communism.

Should it be possible to continue conscription beyond any reasonable time by promoting unpopular wars and other means, the draft can always stand as a further barrier to the progress of youth in life, destroying any immediate hope to participate in his nation's civil life.

By these means the patriotism of youth for their Capitalistic flag can be dulled to a point where they are no longer dangerous as soldiers. While this might require many decades to effect, Capitalism's short-term view will never envision the lengths across which we can plan.

---

[76] A child who is forbidden to work will feel himself to be useless, and will rebel. This is a known fact in the field of Dianetics.

[77] A child, who feels that he is not contributing to his family, Country, or society, will come to resent them.

[78] Pornography is ubiquitous in our culture, and the Internet is a sewer of sexual depravity.

[79] "Sexpol" - Meaning is unknown - so in original.

If we could effectively kill the national pride and patriotism of just one generation we will have won that country.[80] Therefore there must be continual propaganda abroad to undermine the loyalty of the citizens in general and the teenager in particular.

The role of the Psychopolitical operator in this is very strong. He can, from his position as an authority on the mind, advise all manner of destructive measures. He can teach the lack of control of this child at home. He can instruct in an optimum situation the entire nation and how to handle children[81] – and instruct them so that the children, given no control, given no real home, can run wildly about with no responsibility for their nation or themselves.

The misalignment of the loyalty of youth to a Capitalistic nation sets the proper stage for a realignment of their loyalties with Communism. Creating a greed[82] for drugs, sexual misbehavior and uncontrolled freedom and presenting this to them as a benefit of Communism will with ease bring about our alignment.

In the case of strong leaders amongst youthful groups, a Psychopolitical operator can work in many ways to use or discard that leadership. If it is to be used, the character of the girl or boy must be altered carefully into criminal channels and a control by blackmail or other means must be maintained. But where the leadership is not susceptible; where it resists all persuasions and might become dangerous to our cause, no pains must be spared to direct the attention of the authorities to that person and to harass him in one way or another until he can come into the hands of juvenile authorities. When this has been effected it can be hoped that a Psychopolitical operator, by reason of child adviser status can, in the security of the jail and cloaked by

---

[80] Many of the youth today, do not even have a cursory knowledge of our history. When polled, a great majority of students never heard of Pearl Harbor, the Holocaust, JFK, Korea, Vietnam, or other major events in our history.

[81] This is certainly true, as many books on child-rearing and child behavior have been written by psychiatrists and psychologists, and other Hick-Farmer-Sigmund-Freud-Wannabes.

[82] "Greed" probably should be "need" – so in original.

processes of law, destroy the sanity of that person.[83] Particularly brilliant scholars, athletes and youth group leaders must be handled in either one of these two ways.

In the matter of guiding the activities of juvenile courts, the Psychopolitical operator entertains here one of his easier tasks. A Capitalistic nation is so filled with injustice in general that a little more passes without comment. In juvenile courts there are always persons with strange appetites whether these be judges or policemen or women. If such do not exist they can be created.

By making available to them young boys or girls in the "security" of the jail or the detention home, and by appearing with flash cameras[84] or witnesses, one becomes equipped with a whip adequate to direct all the future decisions of that person when these are needed.

The handling of youth cases by courts should be led further and further away from law and further and further into "mental problems" until the entire nation thinks of "mental problems" instead of criminals.[85] This places vacancies everywhere in the courts, in the offices of District Attorneys and, on police staffs which could then be filled with Psychopolitical operators, who become then the judges of the land by their influence and into their hands comes the total control of the criminal, without whose help a revolution cannot ever be accomplished.

By stressing this authority over the problems of youth and adults in courts one day the demand for Psychopolitical operators could become such that even the armed services will use "authorities on the

---

[83] Sexual abuse in prisons is ubiquitous in United States. a tragic example of this is the life of Jack Henry Abbott-author of "In the Belly of the Beast", who was raised by State institutions since the age of twelve, and later in prison, and ended up committing suicide at Wendy Correctional Facility, in Alden, New York in 2001.

[84] Writing over 50 years ago, you can just imagine what Mr. Stickley would have proposed to be done with today's microchip video camera technology!

[85] This has long-since been done in the United States, as prisoners and convicts are routinely referred to as "inmates".

41

mind" to work their various justices and when this occurs the armed forces of the nation then enter into our hands as solidly as if we commanded them ourselves.[86] With the slight bonus of having thus a skilled interrogator near every technician or handler of secret war apparatus, the country, in event of revolution, as did Germany in 1918 and 1919, will find itself immobilized by its own Army and Navy fully and entirely in Communist hands.

Thus the subject of loyalties and realignment is in fact subject of non-armed conquest of an enemy.

---

[86] Our military and CIA have long-since had "Psy-Ops" divisions whose purpose is propaganda and indoctrination of troops – our own as well as the enemy's.

CHAPTER VI
THE GENERAL SUBJECT OF OBEDIENCE

Obedience is the result of force.[87]

Everywhere we look in the history of Earth we discover that obedience to new rulers has come about entirely through the demonstration on the part of those rulers of greater force than was to be discovered in the old ruler. A population overridden, conquered by war, is obedient to its conqueror. It is obedient to its conqueror because its conqueror has exhibited more force.

Concurrent with force is brutality; for there are human considerations involved which also represent force. The most barbaric, unrestrained, brutal use of force, if carried far enough, invokes obedience. Savage force, sufficiently long displayed toward any individual, will bring about his concurrence with any principal or order.

Force is the antithesis of humanizing actions. It is also synonymous in the human mind with savageness, lawlessness, brutality, and barbarism that it is only necessary to display an inhumane attitude toward people, to be granted by those people the possession of force.

Any organization, which has the spirit and courage to display inhumanity, savageness, brutality, and an uncompromising lack of humanity, will be obeyed. Such a use of force is itself, the essential ingredient of greatness. We have to hand no less an example that our great Communist Leaders, who, in moments of duress and trial, when faced by Czarist rule, continued over the heads of an enslaved populace, yet displayed sufficient courage never to stay their hands in the execution of the conversion of the Russian State to Communist rule.

---

[87] Applying coercion instills resentment, and upon opportunity, a person who has not been driven to apathy, will rebel.

43

If you would have obedience you must have no compromise with humanity. If you would have obedience you must make it clearly understood that you have no mercy. Man is an animal.[88] He understands, in the final analysis, only those things that a brute understands.

As an example of this, we find an individual refusing to obey, and being struck. His refusal to obey is now less vociferous. He is struck again, and his resistance is lessened once more. He is hammered and pounded again and again, until, at length, his only thought is direct and implicit obedience to that person from whom the force has emanated. This is a proven principle.

This is a proven principle. It is proven because it is the main principle Man, the animal, has used since his earliest beginnings. It is the only principle that has been effective, the only principle that has brought about a wide and continued belief. For it is to our benefit that an individual who was struck again and again and again from a certain source, will, at length, hypnotically believe anything he is told by the source of the blows.

The stupidity of Western civilizations is best demonstrated by the fact that they believe hypnotism is a thing of the mind, of attention, and a desire for unconsciousness. This is not true. Only when a person has been beaten, punished, and mercilessly hammered, can hypnotism upon him be guaranteed in its effectiveness.[89] It is stated by Western authorities on hypnosis that only some 20 per cent[90] of the people are

---

[88] Of course, the "author" of this is in a position to judge "Man"; he been the exception to his own rule, is about all of us "animals". The tenet that "man is an animal", is ubiquitous in the field of psychology.

[89] Physical trauma opens the "core" to the reactive mind, whereby engrams can be inflicted. This is not "hypnosis" *per se*, but conditioning. It is by brutality that man can be made to react as "an animal". What is being described here is what L. Ron Hubbard called "pain-drug hypnosis".

[90] "Per cent" should be "percent" – so in original.

susceptible to hypnotism.[91] This statement is very untrue. Given enough punishment, all of the people in any time and place are susceptible to hypnotism. In other words, by adding force, hypnotism is made uniformly effective. Where unconsciousness could not be induced by simple concentration upon the hypnotist, unconsciousness can be induced by drugs, by blows, by electric shock, and by other means. And where unconsciousness cannot be induced so as to make an implantation or an hypnotic command effective, it is only necessary to amputate the functioning portions of the animal Man's brain to render him null and void and no longer a menace.[92] Thus, we find that hypnotism is entirely effective.

The mechanisms of hypnotism demonstrate clearly that people can be made to believe in certain conditions, and even in their environment or in politics, by the administration of force. Thus, it is necessary for a Psychopolitician to be an expert in the administration of forces. Thus, he can bring about implicit obedience, not only on the part of individual members of the populace, but on the entire populace itself and its government. He need only take unto himself a sufficiently savage role, a sufficiently uncompromising inhuman attitude, and he will be obeyed and believed.

The subject of hypnotism is a subject of belief. What can people be made to believe? They can be made to believe anything that is administered to them with sufficient brutality and force. The obedience of a populace is as good as they will believe.[93]

Despicable religions, such as Christianity, knew this. They knew that if enough faith could be brought into being, a populace could

---

[91] It is true that the majority of people are immune to hypnosis. The higher the tone of the individual, the more immune to suggestion by hypnosis he becomes.

[92] This is commonly done with an operation called "transorbital leucotomy".

[93] Fragmented sentence – so in original.

be enslaved by the Christian mockeries of humanity and mercy,[94] and thus could be disarmed. But one need not count upon this act of faith to bring about a broad belief. One must only exhibit enough force, enough inhumanity, enough brutality and savageness to create implicit belief and therefore and thereby implicit obedience. As Communism is a matter of belief, its study is a study of force.

The earliest Russian psychiatrists, pioneering the science of psychiatry, understood thoroughly that hypnosis is induced by acute fear. They discovered it could also be induced by shock of an emotional nature, and also by extreme privation, as well as by blows and drugs.

In order to induce a high State of hypnogogy[95] in an individual, a group, or a population, an element of terror must always be present on the part of those who would govern. The psychiatrist is aptly suited to this role, for his brutalities are committed in the name of science and are inexplicably complex, and entirely out of view of the human understanding. A sufficient popular terror of the psychiatrist will, in itself, bring about insanity on the part of many individuals.

A Psychopolitical operative, then, can, entirely cloaked with authority, commence and continue a campaign of propaganda, describing various "treatments" which are administered to the insane. A Psychopolitical operative should at all times insist that these treatments are therapeutic and necessary. He can, in all of his literature and his books, list large numbers of pretended cures by these means. But these "cures" need not actually produce any recovery from a state of disturbance. As long as the Psychopolitical operative or his dupes are the only authorities as to the difference between sanity and insanity, their word as to the therapeutic value of such treatment will be the final word. No layman

---

[94] Faith in God frees a man to become self-determined. It imposes no compulsion other than the will of the Creator. It inspires in its unadulterated practice, the love of fellow man, and peace among nations.

[95] Hypnogogy - Sleepiness, or the State of near-exhaustion, where the mind is malleable to suggestion.

would dare adventure to place judgment upon the state of sanity of an individual whom the psychiatrist has already declared insane. The individual himself is unable to complain, and his family, as will be covered later, is already discredited by the occurrence of insanity in their midst. There must be other adjudicators of insanity; otherwise it could be disclosed that the brutalities practiced in the name of treatment are not therapeutic.

A Psychopolitical operative has no interest in "therapeutic means" or "cures". The greater [the] number of insane in the country where he is operating, the larger [the] number of the populace will come under his view and the greater will become his facilities. Because the problem is apparently mounting into uncontrollable heights, he can more and more operate in an atmosphere of emergency, which again excuses his use of such treatments as electric shock, the prefrontal lobotomy, transorbital leucotomy,[96] and other operations long-since practiced in Russia on political prisoners.

It is to the interest of the Psychopolitical operative that the possibility of curing the insane be outlawed and ruled out at all times.[97] For the sake of obedience on the part of the population and their general reaction, a level of brutality must, at all costs, be maintained. Only in this way can the absolute judgment of the Psychopolitical operative as to the sanity or insanity of public figures be maintained in complete belief. Using sufficient brutality upon their patients, the public at large will come to believe utterly anything they say about their patients. Furthermore, and much more important, the field of the mind must be sufficiently dominated by the Psychopolitical operative, so that wherever tenets of the mind are taught they will be hypnotically believed. The Psychopolitical operative, having under his control all psychology classes in an area, can thus bring about a complete

---

[96] The barbarism and cruelty of early psychiatric practices included prefrontal lobotomies, transorbital leucotomy's (destruction of the prefrontal lobe of the brain by inserting a dime store ice pick through the eye socket, and tearing up the front-part of the brain – the frontal lobes - with a scraping motion.)

[97] There is no need to outlaw these things, the technology and methodology of psychology is ineffective in treating even the most trivial of mental problems.

reformation of the future leaders of country in their educational processes, and so prepare them for Communism.

To be obeyed, one must be believed.[98] If one is sufficiently believed, one will unquestioningly be obeyed. When he is fortunate enough to obtain into his hands anyone near to a political or important figure, this factor of obedience becomes very important. A certain amount of fear or terror must be engendered in the person under treatment so that this person will then take immediate orders, completely and unquestioningly, from the Psychopolitical operative, and so be able to influence the actions of that person who is to be reached.

Bringing about this state of mind on the part of a populace and its leaders - that a Psychopolitical operative must, at all times, be believed - could eventually be attended by very good fortune. It is not too much to hope that Psychopolitical operatives would then, in a country such as the United States, become the most intimate advisers to political figures, even to the point of advising the entirety of a political party as to its actions in an election.[99]

The long view is the important view. Belief is engendered by a certain amount of fear and terror from an authoritative level, and this will be followed by obedience.

The general propaganda which would best serve Psychopolitics would be a continual insistence that certain authoritative levels of

---

[98] In order to believe a lie, one first has to stop believing the truth. And once one stops believing the truth, it is possible that he can be made to believe anything.

[99] This Statement is not too far from the truth. Presidents and heads of State have routinely consulted soothsayers, mediums, Ouija boards, crystal balls, tarot cards, and yes, psychologists before making critical decisions affecting the security and future of United States.

healing, deemed this or that the correct treatment on insanity.[100] These treatments must always include a certain amount of brutality.[101]

Propaganda should continue and stress the rising incidence of insanity in a country. The entire field of human behavior, for the benefit of the country, can, at length, be broadened into abnormal behavior. Thus, anyone indulging in any eccentricity, particularly the eccentricity of combating Psychopolitics could be silenced by the authoritative opinion on the part of the Psychopolitical operative that he was acting in an abnormal fashion.[102] This, with some good fortune, could bring the person into the hands of the Psychopolitical operative so as to forever more disable him or to swerve his loyalties by pain-drug hypnotism.

On the subject of obedience itself, the most optimum obedience is unthinking obedience. The command given must be obeyed without any rationalizing on the part of the subject.[103] The command must, therefore, be implanted below the thinking processes of the subject to be influenced, and must react upon him in such a way as to bring no mental alertness on his part.[104] It is in the interest of Psychopolitics that a population be told that a hypnotized person will not do anything against his actual will, will not commit immoral acts, and will not act so as to endanger himself. While this may be true of light, parlor hypnotism, it certainly is not true of commands implanted with the use of electric shock, drugs, or heavy punishment.[105] It is counted upon completely that this will be discredited to the general public by Psychopolitical operatives, for if it were to be generally known that

---

[100] The bewildering arrays of "treatment" methodologies developed by psychiatrists are all ineffective. Each Ph.D. must complete a thesis, and that thesis expounds a new methodology or technique for "treatment".

[101] In modern times, brutality has surrendered its place to coercion and intimidation.

[102] The DSM-IV has a category of "mental disorder", described as "resistance to treatment".

[103] This, in some measure, is part of military combat training. A person who thinks too much about what he is doing, except killing the enemy, is likely to be killed in combat.

[104] This describes the action of an engram; a person is unaware that engrams even exist.

[105] This is called "pain-drug" hypnosis.

individuals would obey commands harmful to themselves, and would commit immoral acts while under the influence of deep hypnotic commands, the actions of many people, working unknowingly in favor of Communism, would be too-well understood. People acting under hypnotic commands should be acting apparently of their own volition and out of their own convictions.

The entire subject of Psychopolitical hypnosis, Psychopolitics in general, depends for its defence upon continuous protest from authoritative sources that such things are not possible. And, should anyone unmask a Psychopolitical operative, he should at once declare the whole thing a physical impossibility, and use his authoritative position to discount any accusation. Should any writings of Psychopolitics come to view, it is only necessary to brand them a hoax and laugh them out of countenance. Thus, Psychopolitical activities are easy to defend.

When Psychopolitical activities have reached a certain peak, from there on it is almost impossible to undo them, for the population is already under the duress of obedience to the Psychopolitical operatives and their dupes. The ingredient of obedience is important, for the complete belief in the Psychopolitical operative renders his statement canceling any challenge about Psychopolitical operatives irrefutable. The optimum circumstances would be to occupy every position that would be consulted by officials on any question or suspicion arising on the subject of Psychopolitics. Thus, a psychiatric adviser should be placed near to hand in every government operation.[106] As all suspicions would then be referred to him, no action would ever be taken, and the goal of Communism could be realized in that nation.

---

[106] Psychiatrists, psychologists, social workers, and every iteration of unqualified and un-credentialed "Hick-Farmer-Sigmund-Freud-Wannabes", are ubiquitous in our schools, in the prisons, in the government, and in this society in general. Dangerous psychotropic drugs are routinely given to schoolchildren, and advertised on television.

Psychopolitics depends, from the viewpoint of the layman, upon its fantastic aspects. These are its best defence,[107] but above all these defences is implicit obedience on the part of officials and the general public, because of the character of the Psychopolitical operative in the field of healing.

---

[107] Defence – (archaic form) – "defense".

CHAPTER VII
ANATOMY OF STIMULUS-RESPONSE MECHANISM OF MAN

Man is a stimulus-response animal.[108] His entire reasoning capabilities even his ethics and morals depend upon stimulus-response machinery. This has long been demonstrated by such Russians as Pavlov,[109] and principles have long been used in handling the recalcitrant, in training children,[110] and in bringing about a State of optimum behavior on the part of a population.

Having no independent will of his own,[111] Man is easily handled by stimulus response mechanisms. It is only necessary to install a stimulus into the mental anatomy of Man to have that stimulus reactivate and respond any time an exterior command source calls it into being.[112]

The mechanisms of stimulus-response are easily understood. The body {Reactive Mind} takes pictures of every action in the environment around an individual.[113] When the environment includes brutality, terror, shock, and other such activities, the mental image picture[114] gained contains in itself all the ingredients of the environment. If the individual, himself, was injured during that moment, the injury itself will re-manifest when called upon to respond by an exterior command source.

---

[108] This is a major tenant of psychiatry and psychology. It is not true.

[109] Who experimented with salivating dogs.

[110] "Training" – as in using non-existent "disorders" such as "AH/ADD" and prescribing a host of dangerous psychotropic pharmacology to 9 million children in the USA.

[111] Psychiatry really believes this.

[112] This can be and external command source, or similarities in the current environment that approximate conditions that existed when the trauma was inflicted.

[113] In Dianetics, this is called "The Time Track".

[114] Mental Image Pictures are stored for every moment of a person's life, from conception to death. In Scientology this is called "The Time Track". it is interesting that the alleged author Charles Stickley used Dianetics phraseology in this 1955 tome.

As an example of this, if an individual is beaten, and is told during the entirety of the beating that he must obey certain officials, he will, in the future, feel the beginnings of the pain in the moment he begins to disobey.[115] The installed pain itself reacts as a policeman, for the experience of the individual demonstrates to him that he cannot combat, and will receive pain from, certain officials.

The mind can become very complex in its stimulus responses.[116] As easily demonstrated in hypnotism, an entire chain of commands, having to do with a great many complex actions, can be beaten, shocked, or terrorized into a mind, and will there lie dormant until called into view by some similarity in the circumstances of the environment to the incident of punishment. {This is the known mechanism that operates in the case of "flashbacks"in people suffering Post-Traumatic Stress Disorder}.

The stimulus we call the "incident of punishment" where the response mechanism need only contain some small part of the stimulus to call into view the mental image picture, and cause it to exert against the body the pain sequence. So long as the individual obeys the picture, or follows the commands of the stimulus implantation, he is free from pain.

The behavior of children is regulated in this fashion in every civilized country. The father, finding himself unable to bring about immediate obedience and training on the part of his child, resorts to physical violence, and after administering punishment of a physical nature to the child on several occasions, is gratified to experience

---

[115] This is true – restimulation of an engram often raises the original somatic.

[116] Actually, the reactive mind only seems complex; it is the absence of context in the reactive mind, which causes confusion, which appears to be complexity to someone not trained in Dianetics.

complete obedience on the part of the child each time the father speaks. In that parents are wont to be lenient with their children, they seldom administer sufficient punishment to bring about entirely optimum obedience. The ability of the organism to withstand punishment is very great. Complete and implicit response can be gained only by stimuli sufficiently brutal to actually injure the organism. The Cossack method of breaking wild horses is a useful example. The horse will not restrain itself or take any of the rider's commands. The rider, wishing to break it, mounts, and takes a flask of strong Vodka, and smashes it between the horse's ears. The horse, struck to its knees, its eyes filled with alcohol, mistakes the dampness for blood, instantly and thereafter gives its attention to the rider and never needs further breaking. Difficulty in breaking horses is only occasioned when light punishments are administered. There is some mawkish sentimentality about "breaking the spirit", but what is desired here is an obedient horse, and sufficient brutality brings about an obedient horse.

The stimulus-response mechanisms of the body are such that the pain and the command subdivide so as to counter each other. The mental image picture of the punishment will not become effective upon the individual unless the command content is disobeyed. It is pointed out in many early Russian writings that this is a survival mechanism. It has already been well and thoroughly used in the survival of Communism.

It is only necessary to deliver into the organism a sufficient stimulus to gain an adequate response.

So long as the organism obeys the stimulus whenever it is restimulated in the future, it does not suffer from the pain of the stimulus. But should it disobey the command content of the stimulus, the stimulus reacts to punish the individual. Thus, we have an optimum circumstance, and one of the basic principles of Psychopolitics. A sufficiently installed stimulus will thereafter remain as a police mechanism within the individual to cause him to follow commands and directions given to him. Should he fail to follow these commands and directions, the stimulus mechanism will go into action. As the commands are there with the moment of duress, the commands themselves need never be repeated, and if the individual were to depart thousands of miles away from the Psychopolitical operative, he will still obey the Psychopolitical operative, or, himself, become extremely ill and in agony.

These principles, built from the earliest days of Pavlov, by constant and continuous Russian development, have, at last, become of enormous use to us in our conquest. For less modern and well-informed countries of Earth, lacking this mechanism, failing to understand it, and coaxed into somnolence[117] by our own Psychopolitical operatives, who discount and disclaim it, cannot avoid succumbing to it.

The body is less able to resist the stimulus if it has insufficient food and is weary. Therefore, it is necessary to administer all such stimuli to individuals when their ability to resist has been reduced by privation and exhaustion. Refusal to let them sleep over many days, denying them adequate food, then brings about an optimum state for the receipt of a stimulus.[118] If the person is then given an electric shock, and is told while the shock is in action that he must obey and do certain things, he has no choice but to do them, or to re-experience, because of his mental image picture of it, the electric shock. This highly scientific and intensely workable mechanism cannot be overestimated in the practice of Psychopolitics.

During the {shock treatment} the individual produces an artificial exhaustion, and if he is drugged, or shocked and beaten, and given a string of commands, his loyalties, themselves, can be definitely rearranged. This is P. D. H., or Pain Drug Hypnosis.

---

[117] Somnolence - Sleepiness, drowsiness
[118] This was a common technique used by the Unification Church to brainwash its members.

The Psychopolitical operative in training should be thoroughly studied in the subject of hypnotism and post hypnotic suggestion. He should pay particular attention to the "forgetter mechanism"[119] aspect of hypnotism, which is to say, implantation in the unconscious mind. He should note particularly that a person given a command in hypnotic state, and then told when still in that condition to forget it, will execute it {execute the command} on a stimulus-response signal in the environment after he has "awakened" from his hypnotic trance.

Having mastered these details fully, he {the Psychopolitical Operative} should, by practicing upon criminals and prisoners or inmates available to him,[120] produce hypnotic trance by drugs, and drive home post-hypnotic suggestions by pain administered to the drugged person. He should then study the reactions of the person when "awakened", and should give him the stimulus- response signal that would throw into action the commands given while in the drugged state of duress. By much practice he can then learn the threshold dosages of various drugs, and the amount of duress in terms of electric shock or additional drug shock necessary to produce the optimum obedience to the commands. He should also satisfy himself that there is no possible method known to Man - there must be no possible method known to man - of bringing the patient into awareness of what has happened to him, keeping him in a state of obedience and response while ignorant of its cause.

Using criminals and prisoners, the Psychopolitical-operative-in-training should then experiment with duress in the absence of privation, administering electric shocks, beatings, and terror inducing tactics, accompanied by the same mechanisms as those employed in

---

[119] "forgetter mechanism" is a term used in Dianetics and Scientology, which describes the portion of an engram that commands the mind to forget and experience.

[120] Experimentation on prisoners is nothing new; it is still practiced in New York prisons to this day. See "Prisoner Abuse" articles on my web site at www.Net4TruthUSA.com/PrisonerAbuse.htm

hypnotism, and watch the conduct of the person when {he is} no longer under duress.

The operative in training should carefully remark those who show a tendency to protest, so that he may recognize possible recovery of memory of the commands implanted. Purely for his own education, he should then satisfy himself as to the efficacy of brain surgery in disabling the non-responsive prisoner. The boldness of the Psychopolitical operative can be increased markedly by permitting persons who have been given pain drug hypnosis and have demonstrated symptoms of rebelling, or recalling into society to observe how the label of "insanity" discredits and discounts the statements of the person.

Exercises in bringing about insanity seizures at will, simply by demonstrating a signal to persons upon whom pain drug hypnosis has been used, and exercises in making the seizures come about through talking to certain persons in certain places and times should also be used.

Brain surgery, as developed in Russia, should also be practiced by the Psychopolitical operative in training, to give him full confidence in (1) The crudeness with which it can be done, (2) The certainty of erasure of the stimulus-response mechanism itself, (3) The production imbecility, idiocy, and dis-coordination on the part of the patient, and (4) The small amount of comment which casualties in brain surgery occasion.

Exercises in sexual attack on patients should be practiced by the Psychopolitical operative to demonstrate the inability of the patient under pain-drug-hypnosis to recall the attack,[121] while indoctrinating a lust for further sexual activity on the part of the patient.

---

[121] If the reader doubts that this actually happens, see: www.cchr.org and links from my web site at: www.net4TruthUSA.com/CCHRLinks.htm

Sex, in all animals, is a powerful motivator, and is no less so in the animal Man, and the occasioning of sexual liaison between females of a target family and indicated males,[122] under the control of the Psychopolitical operative, must be demonstrated to be possible with complete security for the Psychopolitical operative, thus giving into his hands an excellent weapon for the breaking down of familial relations and consequent public disgraces for the Psychopolitical target.

Just as a dog can be trained, so can a man be trained. Just as a horse can be trained, so can a man be trained. Sexual lust, masochism, and any other desirable perversion can be induced by pain-drug-hypnosis[123] and the benefit of Psychopolitics. The changes of loyalties, allegiances, and sources of command can be occasioned easily by Psychopolitical technologies, and these should be practiced and understood by the Psychopolitical operative before he begins to tamper with Psychopolitical targets of magnitude.

The actual simplicity of the subject of pain-drug-hypnosis, the use of electric shock, drugs, insanity-producing injections, and other materials, should be masked entirely by technical nomenclature, by the protest of benefit to the patient, by an authoritarian pose and position, and by carefully cultivating governmental positions in the country to be conquered.

Although the Psychopolitical operative working in universities where he can direct the curricula of psychology classes is often tempted to teach some of the principal of Psychopolitics to the susceptible students in the psychology classes, he must be thoroughly enjoined to limit his information in psychology classes to the transmittal of the

---

[122] These "sexual liaisons" are implied as abuse of "professional" status, as many perverts seek positions in the "mental healing" professions, because if an accusation arises, they can always claim that their patients "are insane" or "just making it up". See: www.cchr.org or www.freedommag.org. Literature links are provided on www.Net4TruthUSA.comCCHRLinks.htm

[123] Perversion can be induced by an inflicted trauma, which the victim then unwittingly succumbs to, by adopting the valence of the attacker in order to become "cause over effect".

tenets of Communism under the guise of psychology, and must limit his activities in bringing about a state of mind on the part of the students where they will accept Communist tenets as those of their own action and as modern scientific principles. The psychological operative must not, at any time, educate students fully in stimulus-response mechanisms, and must not impart to them, save those who will become his fellow workers, the exact principles of Psychopolitics. It is not necessary to do so, and it is dangerous.

CHAPTER VIII
DEGRADATION, SHOCK, AND ENDURANCE

Degradation and conquest are companions.

In order to be conquered, a nation must be degraded, either by acts of war, by being overrun, by being forced into humiliating treaties of peace, or by the treatment of her populace under the armies of the conqueror. However, degradation can be accomplished much more insidiously and much more effectively by consistent and continual defamation.

Defamation is the best and foremost weapon of Psychopolitics on the broad field. Continual and constant degradation of national leaders, national institutions, national practices, and national heroes must be systematically carried out, but this is the chief function of the Communist Party Members, in general, not the Psychopolitician.

The realm of defamation and degradation, of the Psychopolitician, is Man himself. By attacking the character and morals of Man himself, and by bringing about, through contamination of youth, a general degraded feeling, command of the populace is facilitated to a very marked a degree.

There is a curve of degradation, which leads downward to a point where the endurance of an individual is almost at an end, and any sudden action toward him will place him in a State of shock. Similarly, a soldier held prisoner can be abused, denied, defamed, and degraded until the slightest motion on the part of his captors will cause him to flinch. Similarly, the slightest word on the part of his captors will cause him to obey, or vary his loyalties and beliefs. Given sufficient degradation, a prisoner can be caused to murder his fellow countrymen in the same stockade.[124] Experiments on German prisoners have lately demonstrated that only after seventy days of filthy food, little sleep, and nearly untenable quarters, that the least motion toward the prisoner would bring about a state of shock beyond his endurance threshold, and would cause him to hypnotically receive anything said to him. Thus, it is possible, in an entire stockade of prisoners, to the number of thousands, to bring about a state of complete servile obedience, and without the labor of personally addressing each one, to pervert their loyalties and implant in them adequate commands to insure[125] their future conduct, even when released to their own people.

By lowering the endurance of a person, a group, or a nation, and by constant degradation and defamation, it is possible to induce, thus, a state of shock that will receive adequately any command given.

The first thing to be degraded in any nation is the state of man himself. Nations that have high ethical tone[126] are difficult to conquer. Their loyalties are hard to shake, their allegiance to their leaders is fanatical, and what they usually call their "spiritual integrity" cannot be violated by duress. It is not efficient to attack a nation in such a frame of mind. It is the basic purpose of Psychopolitics to reduce that state of mind to a point where it can be ordered and enslaved.

Thus, the first target is Man himself. He must be degraded from a spiritual being to an animalistic reaction pattern. He must think of himself as an animal, capable only of animalistic reactions.[127] He must no longer think of himself, or his fellows, as capable of "spiritual endurance", or nobility.

---

[124] Prisoner-on-prisoner assaults, murders, and rapes, are ubiquitous in US prisons. The NEWS media never reports these things to the public; politicians would find it too embarrassing.

[125] "Insure" should be "ensure" – so in original.

[126] "High ethical tone" is Dianetics / Scientology terminology. A "high ethical tone" means that the individual or nation has an acute perception of what is right and wrongs; a concern for the greater good of other individuals, his/her family, community, country, and the brotherhood of mankind.

[127] This is the main purpose of teaching the theory of evolution – which is a Pagan religion – in the public schools.

The best approach toward degradation in its first stages is the propaganda of "scientific approach" to Man. Man must be consistently demonstrated to be a mechanism without individuality, and it must be educated into a populace under attack that Man's individualistic reactions are the product of mental derangement. The populace must be brought into the belief that every individual within it who rebels in any way, shape, or form against efforts and activities to enslave the whole, must be considered to be a deranged person whose eccentricities are neurotic or insane, and who must have at once the treatment of a Psychopolitician.

An optimum condition in such a programme[128] of degradation would address itself to the military forces of the nation, and bring them rapidly away from any other belief than that the disobedient one must be subjected to "mental treatment". An enslavement of a population can fail only if these rebellious individuals are left to exert their individual influences upon their fellow citizens, sparking them into rebellion, calling into account their nobilities and freedoms. Unless these restless individuals are stamped out and given into the hands of Psychopolitical operatives early in the conquest, they will be nothing but trouble as the conquest continues.[129]

The officials of the government, students, readers, partakers of entertainment, must all be indoctrinated, by whatever means, into the complete belief that the restless, the ambitious, the natural leaders, are suffering from environmental maladjustments, which can only be healed by recourse to Psychopolitical operatives in the guise of mental healers.

---

[128] Archaic form: program (so in original)
[129] I intend to be "nothing but trouble" to the Psychopoliticians and their unwitting dupes in the media – WebPastor Dave T.

By thus degrading the general belief in the status of Man, it is relatively simple, with the cooperation from the economic salients[130] being driven into the country, to drive citizens apart, one from another, to bring about a question of the wisdom of their own government,[131] and to cause them to actively beg for enslavement.

The educational programmes[132] of Psychopolitics must, at every hand, seek out the levels of youth who will become the leaders in the country's future, and educate them into the belief in the animalistic nature of Man.[133] This must be made fashionable. They must be taught above all things that the salvation of Man is to be found only by his adjusting thoroughly to this environment.[134] This educational programming the field of Psychopolitics can best be followed by bringing about a compulsory training in some subject such a psychology or other mental practice, and ascertaining that each broad programme of Psychopolitical training be supervised by a psychiatrist who is a trained Psychopolitical operative.

As it seems in foreign nations that the church is the most ennobling influence, each and every branch and activity of each and every church, must, one way or another, be discredited. Religion must become unfashionable by demonstrating broadly, through Psychopolitical indoctrination, that the soul is nonexistent, and that Man is an animal.[135]

---

[130] Salient – standing out in a way that compels attention – no plural form – so in original.

[131] "Wisdom in government" is an oxymoron; a non-sequituer.

[132] Archaic form: Programs – so in original.

[133] This is the prime tenet of psychology; Man is an animal – sans this belief, Communism crumbles.

[134] Precisely the opposite is true. A man is only a sane as he adjusts his environment to him. His "salvation" consists of his acceptance of the fact that his mere physical existence is not all there is. Adjusting to an environment is a State of apathy, which leads to death.

[135] Religion is under attack by evolutionist humanists. They are the ones that contend that "man is animal", and denied the existence of a soul.

The lying mechanisms of Christianity lead men to foolishly brave deeds. By teaching them that there is a life hereafter, the liability of courageous acts, while living, is thus lessened.[136] The liability of any act must be markedly increased if a populace is to be obedient. Thus there must be no standing belief in the church, and the power of the church of must be denied at every hand.

The Psychopolitical operative, in his programme of degradation, should at all times bring into question any family which is deeply religious, and, should any neurosis or insanity be occasioned in that family, to blame and hold responsible their religious connections for the neurotic or psychotic condition. Religion must be made synonymous with neurosis and psychosis. People who are deeply religious would be less and less held responsible for their own sanity, and should more and more be relegated to the ministrations of Psychopolitical operatives.

By perverting the institutions of a nation and bringing about a general degradation, by interfering with the economics of a nation to the degree that privation and depression come about, only minor shocks will be necessary to produce, on the populace as a whole, an obedient reaction or an hysteria. Thus, the mere threat of war, the mere threat of aviation bombings, could cause the population to sue instantly for peace.[137] It is a long and arduous road for the Psychopolitical operative to achieve the state of mind on the part of a whole nation, but no more than twenty or thirty years should be necessary in the entire programme; having to hand, as we do, weapons with which to accomplish the goal.

---

[136] Similarly, fundamentalist Muslims are indoctrinated and brainwashed into becoming Jihad suicide bombers or terrorist hijackers.

[137] This is precisely why the government allowed the 9-11 attacks to happen. If the threat is real, ominous, and severe enough, people will give up their money and their liberty, just to feel safe. The Devil said to God in the book of Job, chapter 2: *"...yea, skin for skin, all that a man hath, he will give for his life."*

CHAPTER IX
THE ORGANIZATION OF MENTAL HEALTH CAMPAIGNS

Psychopolitical operatives should at all times be alert to the opportunity to organize "for the betterment of the community" mental health clubs or groups. By thus inviting the cooperation of the population as a whole in mental health programmes, the terrors of mental aberration can be disseminated throughout the populace. Furthermore, each one of these mental health groups properly guided can bring, at last, legislative pressure against the government to secure adequately the position of the Psychopolitical operative, and to obtain for him government grants and facilities, thus bringing a government to finance its own downfall.

Mental health organizations must carefully delete from their ranks anyone actually proficient in handling or treatment of mental health. Thus must be excluded priests, ministers, actually trained psychoanalysts, good hypnotists,[138] or trained ministers of the Church of Scientology. These, with some cognizance on the subject of mental aberration and its treatment, and with some experience in observing the mentally deranged, if allowed frequency within institutions, and if permitted to receive literature, wood, sooner or later, become suspicious of the activities engaged upon by the Psychopolitical operative. These must be defamed and excluded as "untrained", "unskillful", "quacks", or "perpetrators of hoaxes".

No mental health movement with actual goals of mental therapy should be continued in existence in any nation.[139] For instance, the use of Chinese acupuncture in the treatment of mental and physical derangement must, in China, be stamped out and discredited

---

[138] There is no such thing as a "good hypnotist". There is no comparison between the cited professions and a minister in the Church of Scientology whom are all mentioned.

[139] At present, the Chinese government is persecuting the practitioners of Falun Gong, which is essentially a set of meditation and breathing exercises. See links on my web site at: www.Net4TruthUSA.com or www.fofg.org

thoroughly, as it has some efficacy, and, more importantly, its practitioners understand, too long conversation with it, many of the principles of actual mental health and aberration.

In the field of mental health, the Psychopolitician must occupy, and continue to occupy, through various arguments, the authoritative position on the subject. There is always the danger that problems of mental health may be resolved by some individual or group, which might then derange the programme of the Psychopolitical operative in his mental health clubs.

City officials, socialites, and other unknowing individuals, on the subject of mental health, should be invited to full cooperation in the activity of mental health groups. But the entirety of this activity should be to finance better facilities for the Psychopolitical practitioner. To these groups, it must be continually stressed that the entire subject of mental illness is so complex that none of them, certainly, could understand any part of it. Thus, the club should be kept on a social and financial level.

Where groups interested in the health of the community have already been formed, they should be infiltrated and taken over, and if this is not possible, they should be discredited and debarred, and the officialdom of the area should be invited to stamp them out as dangerous. When a hostile group dedicated to mental health is discovered, the Psychopolitician should have recourse to the mechanisms of peyote, mescaline, and later drugs, which cause temporary insanity. He should send persons, preferably those {who are} well under his control, into the mental health group, and invite the group, whether Christian Science or Church of Scientology or other practice, to demonstrate its abilities upon this new person. These, in demonstrating their abilities, will usually act with enthusiasm. Midway in the course of their treatment, a quiet injection of peyote, mescaline, or other drug, or an electric shock, will produce the symptoms of insanity in the patient that has been sent to the target group.[140] The patient thus demonstrating momentary insanity should immediately be reported to the police and taken away to some area of incarceration managed by Psychopolitical operatives, and so placed out of sight. Officialdom will thus come into a belief that this group drives individuals insane by their practices, and the practices of the group will then be despised and prohibited by law.

The values of a widespread mental health organization are manifest when one realizes that any government can be forced to provide facilities for Psychopolitical operatives in the form of psychiatric wards in hospitals, and national institutions {that are} totally in the hands of psychological operatives, and the establishment of clinics where youth can be contacted and arranged more seemingly to the purposes of Psychopolitics.

Such groups form a political force, which can then legalize any law or authority desired for the Psychopolitical operative.

The securing of authority over such mental health organizations is done mainly by appeal to education. A Psychopolitical operative should make sure that those psychiatrists he controls; those psychologists, whom he has under his orders, have been trained for an excessively long period of time. The longer the training period which can be required, the safer the Psychopolitical programme {the better}, since no new group of practitioners can arise to disclose {the techniques taught in these}[141] and dismay[142] Psychopolitical programmes. Furthermore, the groups themselves cannot hope to obtain any full knowledge of the subject, not having behind them many, many years of intensive training.

---

[140] The author here fails to mention how "a quiet injection" or an electric shock can be administered to this subject while (presumably) this experiment is being monitored.

[141] Sentence is a fragment – so in original (brackets mine).

[142] The meaning of "dismay" in this context is unclear – so in original.

Vienna has been carefully maintained as the home of Psychopolitics, since it was the home of Psychopolitics, since it was the home of Psychoanalysis. Although our activities have long, long since dispersed any of the gains made by Freudian groups, and have taken over these groups, the proximity of Vienna to Russia, where Psychopolitics is operating abroad, and the necessity "for further study" by Psychopolitical operatives in the birthplace of psychoanalysis, makes periodic contacts with headquarters possible. Thus, the word "psychoanalysis" must be stressed at all times, and must be pretended to be a thorough part of the psychiatrist's training.

Psychoanalysis has the very valuable possession of a vocabulary, and workability, which is sufficiently poor to avoid the recovery of Psychopolitical implantations. It can be made fashionable throughout mental health organizations, and by learning its patter, and by believing they see some of its phenomena, the members of mental health groups can believe themselves conversant with mental health. Because its stress is sex, it is, itself, an adequate defamation of character, and serves the purposes of degradation well. Thus, in organizing mental health groups, the literature furnished such groups should be Psychopolitical in nature.

If a group of persons interested in suppressing juvenile delinquency, in caring for the insane, and the promotion of Psychopolitical operatives and their actions can be formed in every major city of a country under conquest, the success of a Psychopolitical programme is assured, since these groups seem to represent a large segment of the population. By releasing continued propaganda on the subject of dope addiction, homosexuality, and depraved conduct on the part of the young, even the judges of a country can become suborned into reacting violently against the youth of the country, thus mis-aligning and aligning the support of youth.

The communication lines of Psychopolitics, if such mental health organizations can be well established, can thus run from its most prominent citizens to its government. It is not too much in the hope that the influence of such groups could bring about a psychiatric ward in every hospital in the land,[143] and psychiatrists in every company and regiment of the nation's army, and whole government institutes manned entirely by Psychopolitical operatives, into which ailing government officials could be placed, to the advantage of the Psychopolitician.

If a psychiatric ward could be established in every hospital in every city in a nation, it is certain that, at one time or another, every prominent citizen of that nation could come under the ministrations of Psychopolitical operatives or their dupes.

The validation of psychiatric position in the Armed Forces and security-minded institutions of the nation under conquest should bring about a flow and a fund of information unlike any other programme that could be conceived. If every pilot who flies a new plane could come under the questioning of a Psychopolitical operative, if the every compiler or planner of military action could thus come under the review of Psychopolitical operatives, the simplicity with which information can be extracted by the use of certain drugs, without the after-knowledge of the soldier, would entirely cripple any overt action toward Communism. If the nation could be educated into turning over to Psychopolitical operatives every recalcitrant or rebellious soldier, it would lose its best fighters. Thus the advantage of mental health organizations can be seen, for these, by exerting an apparent public pressure against the government, can achieve these ends and goals.

The financing of a Psychopolitical operation is difficult unless it is done by the citizens and government. Although vast sums of money can be obtained from private patients, and from relatives who wish persons put away, it is, nevertheless, difficult to obtain millions, unless

---

[143] In large measure, this goal has been reached. There is not one major hospital in the US that lacks a "spin-bin".

the government itself is cooperating.[144] The cooperation of the government to obtain these vast sums of money is best obtained by the organization of mental health groups composed of leading citizens, and who bring their lobbying abilities to bear against the nation's government. Thus can be financed many programmes, which might otherwise have to be laid aside by the Psychopolitician.

The Psychopolitical operative should bend consistent and continual effort toward forming and continuing in action innumerable mental health groups. The Psychopolitical operatives should also spare no expense in smashing out of existence, by whatever means, any actual healing group, such as that of acupuncture in China; such as Christian Science and Church of Scientology in United States; such as Catholicism in Italy and Spain; and the practical psychology groups of England.

{NOTE: Since this book was written, the American Psychiatric Association (APA) has cataloged 347 different "mental disorders" in its catalog, which is called the "Diagnostic Statistical Manual" (DSM-IV). Now in its 4th edition, the DSM lists no cures or treatments for any of these "disorders", the majority of which are totally bogus (such as "ADD/AHDD", which is a ploy to put over 9 million children in the US on dangerous psychotropic medication. See my web site at www.Net4TruthUSA.com and go to the LINKS pages for current information and links to major anti-psych web sites.

– WebPastor Dave T.}

---

[144] Charles Stickley would be shocked to learn that the US government presently funds billions of dollars in psycho-social experiments and the US military has had "Psy-Ops" divisions for many years.

CHAPTER X
CONDUCT UNDER FIRE

The Psychopolitician may well find himself under attack as an individual or member of a group. He may be attacked as a Communist, through some leak in the organizations; he may be attacked for malpractice. He may be attacked by the families of people whom he has injured. In all cases his conduct of the situation should be calm and aloof. He should have behind him the authority of many years of training, and he should have participated fully in the building of defences[145] in the field of insanity, which give him the only statement as to the conditions of the mind.

If he has not done his work well, hostile feeling groups may expose an individual Psychopolitician. These may call into question the efficacy of psychiatric treatment such a shock, drugs, and brain surgery. Therefore, the Psychopolitical operative must have to hand innumerable documents which assert enormously encouraging figures on the subject of recovery by reason of shock, brain surgery, drugs, and general treatment. Not one of these cases cited need be real, but they should be documented and printed in such a fashion as to form excellent court evidence.

When his allegiance is attacked, the Psychopolitical operative should explain his connection with Vienna on the grounds that Vienna is the place of study for all-important matters of the mind.

More importantly, he should rule into scorn, by reason of his authority, the sanity of the person attacking him, and if the Psychopolitical archives of the country are adequate many defamatory data can be unearthed and presented as a rebuttal.

---

[145] Defences (Archaic form) – Defenses – so in original.

Should anyone attempt to expose psychotherapy as a Psychopolitical activity, the best defence is calling into question the sanity of the attacker. The next best defence is authority. The next best defence is a validation of psychiatric practices in terms of long and aggressive figures. The next best defence is the actual removal of the attacker by giving him, or them, treatment sufficient to bring about a period of insanity for the duration of the trial. This, more than anything else, would discredit them, but it is dangerous to practice this, in the extreme.

Psychopolitics should avoid murder and violence, unless it is done in the safety of the institution, on persons who have been proven to be insane. Where the institution deaths appear to be unnecessary or to rise in "unreasonable number", political capital might be made of this by city officials or legislature. If the Psychopolitical operative has, himself, or if his group has done a thorough job, defamatory data concerning the person, or connections, of the would-be attacker should be on file, should be documented, and should be used in such a way as to discourage the inquiry.

After a period of indoctrination, a country will expect insanity to be met with Psychopolitical violence. Psychopolitical activities should become the only recognized treatment for insanity. Indeed, this can be extended to such a length that could be made illegal for electric shock and brain surgery to be omitted in the treatment of a patient.

In order to defend Psychopolitical activities, a great complexity should be made of psychiatric, psychoanalytical, and psychological technology. Any hearing should be burdened by terminology too difficult to be transcribed easily. A great deal should be made out of such terms as schizophrenia, paranoia, and other relatively indefinable states.

Psychopolitical tests need not necessarily be in agreement, one to another, where they are available to the public. Various types of insanity should be characterized by difficult terms. The actual state should be made obscure, but by this verbiage it can be built into the court or investigating mind that a scientific approach exists and that it is too complex for him to understand. It is not to be imagined that a judge or a committee of investigation should inquire too deeply into the subject of insanity, since they, themselves, part of the indoctrinated masses, are already intimidated if the Psychopolitical activity has caused itself to be well-documented in terms of horror in magazines. In case of a hearing or trial, the terribleness of insanity itself, its threat to the society, should be exaggerated until the court or committee believes that the Psychopolitical operative is vitally necessary in his post and should not be harassed for the activities of persons who are irrational.

An immediate attack upon the sanity of the attacker before any possible hearing can take place is the very best defence. It should become well known that "only the insane attack psychiatrists". The by-word should be built into the society that paranoia is a condition "in which the individual believes he is being attacked by Communists". It will be found that this defence is effective.

Part of the effective defences should include the entire lack in the society of any real psychotherapy. This must be systematically stamped out, since a real psychotherapy might possibly uncover the results of Psychopolitical activities. Jurisprudence, in a Capitalistic nation, is of such clumsiness that cases are invariably tried in their newspapers.[146] We have handled these things much better in Russia,

---

[146] This is so true, that it is impossible to get a fair trial in a high-profile case – especially if the case is sex-related – The Michael Jackson molestation case is a prime example of a media-fueled witch-hunt. See my web site www.Net4TruthUSA.com and bookstore on www.LuLu.com/Net4TruthUSA for psychology-related books. See: www.accused.com for resources for false allegation of child abuse.

and have uniformly brought people to trial with full confessions already arrived at (being implanted)[147] before the trial took place.

Should any whisper, or pamphlet, against Psychopolitical activities be published, it should be laughed to scorn, branded an immediate hoax,[148] and the perpetrator or publisher should be, at the first opportunity, branded as insane, and by the use of drugs the insanity should be confirmed.

---

[147] In the US, some also go to trial with witnesses against them being brainwashed – so that they are absolutely convincing in court. – See above note. You will want to read my books *"The Merchants of Chaos"* and *"The Wheel of Ixion – beyond the Belly of The Beast"*.

[148] The author, allegedly a professor, has poor command of the language; This should be "... immediately branded a hoax.."

CHAPTER XI
THE USE OF PSYCHOPOLITCS IN SPREADING COMMUNISM

Reactionary nations are of such a composition that they attack a word without an understanding of it. As the conquest of a nation by Communism depends upon imbuing its population with Communist tenets, it is not necessary that the term "Communism" be applied at first to the educative measures employed.

As an example, in the United States we have been able to alter the works of William James, and others, into a more acceptable pattern, and to place the tenets of Karl Marx, Pavlov, Lamarck, and the data of Dialectic Materialism into the textbooks of psychology, to such a degree that anyone thoroughly studying psychology becomes at once a candidate to accept the reasonableness of Communism.

As every chair of psychology in the United States is occupied by persons in our connection, or who can be influenced by persons in our connection, the consistent employment of such texts is guaranteed. They are given the authoritative ring, and they are carefully taught.

Constant pressure in the legislatures of the United States can bring about legislation to the effect that every student attending a high school or university must have classes in psychology.

Educating broadly the educated strata of the populace into the tenets of Communism is thus rendered relatively easy, and when the choice is given them whether to continue in a Capitalistic or a Communist condition, they will see, suddenly, in Communism, much more reason ability than in Capitalism, which will now be of our own definition.

CHAPTER XII
VIOLENT REMEDIES

As populaces, in general, understand that of violence is necessary in the handling of the insane, violent remedies seem to be reasonable. Starting from a relatively low level of violence, such as straitjackets and other restraints, is relatively easy to encroach upon the public diffidence for violence by adding more and more cruelty into the treatment of the insane.

By increasing the brutality of "treatment", the public expectance of such treatment will be assisted, and the protest of the individual to whom the treatment is given is impossible, since immediately after the treatment he is incapable. The family of the individual on the treatment is suspect for having in its midst, already, and insane person. The family's protest should be discredited.

The more violent the treatment, the more command out of the Psychopolitical operatives will accumulate. Bring operation should become standard and commonplace. While the figures of actual debts should be repressed wherever possible, nevertheless, it is of no great concern to the Psychopolitical operatives that many deaths do occur.

Gradually, the public should be educated into electric shock,[149] first by believing that it is very therapeutic, then by believing that it is quieting, then by being informed that electric shock usually injures the spine and teeth, and finally, that it very often kills or at least breaks the spine and removes, violently, the teeth of the patient. It is very doubtful if anyone from the lay levels of the public could tolerate the observation of a single electric shock treatment. Certainly they could not tolerate witnessing a prefrontal lobotomy or trans-orbital leucotomy. However they should be brought up to a level where this is

---

[149] "Educated into electric shock"? – So in original.

possible, where it is the expected treatment, and where the details, of the treatment itself can be made known, thus to the increase of Psychopolitical prestige.

The more violent the treatment, the more hopeless insanity will seem to be. The society should be worked up to the level where every recalcitrant young man could be brought into court and assigned to Psychopolitical operative, be given electric shocks, and reduced into unimaginative docility for the remainder of his days.

By continuous and increasing advertising of the violence of treatment, the public will at last come to tolerate the creation of zombie conditions to such a degree that they will probably employ zombies, if given to them. Thus a large strata of the society particularly that, which was rebellious, can be reduced to the service of the Psychopolitician.

By various means, [the] public must be convinced, at least, that insanity can only be met by shock, torture, deprivation, defamation, discreditation,[150] violence, maiming, death, [and] punishment in all its forms. The society, at the same time, must be educated into the belief of increasing insanity within its ranks.[151] This creates an emergency, and places the Psychopolitician in a savior role and places him, at length, in charge of the society.

---

[150] "Discreditation" - No such word – probably means "being discredited" - so in original.

[151] Should read "...belief THAT insanity is increasing within its ranks." – so in original.

CHAPTER XIII
THE RECRUITING OF PSYCHOPOLITICAL DUPES

The Psychopolitical dupe is a well-trained individual who serves in complete obedience to the Psychopolitical operative.

In that nearly all persons in training are expected to undergo a certain amount of treatment in any field of the mind, it is not too difficult to persuade persons in the field of mental healing to subject themselves to mild or minor drugs or shock. If this can be done, a psychological dupe on the basis of pain-drug-hypnosis can immediately result.

Recruitment into the ranks of "mental healing" can best be done by carefully bringing into it, only those healing students who are, to some slight degree, already depraved, or who have been "treated" by Psychopolitical operatives.

Recruitment is effected by making the field of mental healing very attractive, financially, and sexually.

The amount of promiscuity, which can be induced in mental patients, can work definitely to the advantage of the Psychopolitical recruiting agent. The dupe can thus be induced into many lurid sexual contacts, and these, properly witnessed, can thereafter be used as blackmail material to assist any failure of pain-drug-hypnosis in causing him to execute orders.

The promise of unlimited sexual opportunities, the promise of complete dominion over the bodies and minds of helpless patients, the promise of complete lawlessness without detection, can thus attract to "mental healing" many desirable recruits who will willingly fall in line with Psychopolitical activities.

In that the Psychopolitician has under his control the insane of the nation, most of them have criminal tendencies, and as he can, his movement goes forward, recruit for his ranks the criminals themselves, he has unlimited numbers of human beings to employ on whatever project he may see fit. In that the insane will execute destructive projects without question, if given the proper amount of punishment and implantation, the degradation of the country's youth, the defamation of its leaders, the suborning of its courts becomes childishly easy.

The Psychopolitician has the advantage of naming as a delusory symptom any attempt on the part of a patient to expose commands.

The Psychopolitician should carefully adhere to institutions and should eschew private practice whenever possible, since this gives him the greater number of human beings to control [for] the use of Communism. When he does act in private practice, it should be only in contact with the families of the wealthy and the officials of the country.

CHAPTER XIV
THE SMASHING OF RELIGIOUS GROUPS

You must know that until recent times the complete subject of mental derangement, whether so light as simple worry or so heavy as insanity, was the sphere of activity of the church and only the church.

Traditionally in civilized nations and barbaric ones the priesthood alone had in complete charge the mental condition of the citizen. As a matter of great concern to the Psychopolitician this tendency still exists in every public in the Western world and scientific inroads into this sphere has occurred only in official and never in public quarters.

The magnificent tool welded for us by Wundt[152] would be as nothing if it were not for official insistence in civilized countries that "scientific practices" be applied to the problem of the mind. Without this official insistence or even if it relapsed for a moment, the masses would grasp stupidity for the priest, the minister, and the clergy when [their][153] mental condition came in question. Today in Europe and America "scientific practices" in the field of the mind would not last moments if not enforced entirely by officialdom.

It must be carefully hidden that the incidence of insanity has increased only since these "scientific practices" were applied. Great remarks must be made of "the pace of modern living" and other myths as the cause of the increased neurosis in the world. It is nothing to us what causes it if anything does. It is everything to us that no evidence of any kind shall be tolerated afoot to permit the public tendency toward the church its way. If given their heads, if left to themselves to decide, independent of officialdom, where they would place their deranged loved ones; the public would choose religious sanitariums

---

[152] Wundt – an early pioneer of psychiatry.
[153] Sentence is a fragment – so in original (brackets mine).

and would avoid as if plagued places where "scientific practices" prevail.

Given any slightest encouragement, public support would swing on an instant all mental healing into the hands of the churches. And there are churches waiting to receive it, clever churches. That terrible monster of the Roman Catholic Church still dominates mental healing heavily throughout the Christian world and their well-schooled Priests are always at work to turn the public their way. In the field of pure healing the Church of Christ Science of Boston, Massachusetts excels in commanding the public favour and operates many sanitariums. All these must be swept aside. They must be ridiculed and defamed and every cure they advertise must be asserted as a hoax. A full fifth of a Psychopolitician's time should be devoted to smashing these threats. Just as in Russia we had to destroy, after many, many years of the most arduous work, the Church, so we must destroy all faiths in nations marked for conquest.

Insanity must be made to hound the footsteps of every priest and [religious] practitioner. His best results must be turned into jibbering[154] insanities, no matter what means we have to use. You need not care what effect you have upon the public. The effect you care about is the one upon officials. You must recruit every agency of the nation marked for slaughter into a foaming hatred of religious healing. You must suborn District Attorneys and judges into an intense belief as fervent as an ancient faith in God, that Christian Science or any other religious practice which might devote itself to mental healing is vicious, bad, insanity causing, publicly hated and intolerable.

You must suborn and recruit any medical healing organization into collusion in this campaign. You must appeal to their avarice and even their humanity to invite their cooperation in smashing all religious healing and thus, to our end, care of the insane. You must see that such

---

[154] "Jibbering" (possibly slang) – probably means "incoherent babbling" – so in original.

societies have only qualified Communist indoctrines[155] as their advisers in this matter. For you can use such societies. They are stupid and stampede easily. Their cloak and degrees can be used quite well to mask any operation we care to have masked. We must make them partners in our endeavor so that they will never be able to crawl [out] from beneath our thumb and discredit us.

We have battled in America since the century's turn to bring to nothing any and all Christian influences and we are succeeding. While we today seem to be kind to the Christian, remember that we have yet to influence the "Christian world" to our ends. When that is done we shall have an end of them everywhere. You may see them here in Russia as trained apes. They do not know their tether is long only until the apes in other lands have become unwary. You must work until "religion" is synonymous with "insanity". You must work until the officials of city, county and state governments will not think twice before they pounce upon religious groups as public enemies.

Remember [that] all lands are governed by the few and only pretend to consult with the many. It is no different in America. The petty official, the maker of laws alike can be made to believe the worst. It is not necessary to convince the masses. It is only necessary to work in incessantly upon the official, using personal defamations, while the lies, false evidences and constant propaganda to make him fight for you against the church or against any practitioner.

Like the official, the bona fide medical healer also believes the worst if it can be shown to him as dangerous competition. And like the Christian, should he seek to take from us any right we have gained, we shall finish him as well.

We must be like the vine upon the three. We use a tree to climb and then, strangling it, grow into power on the nourishment its flesh.

---

[155] No such word – probably means "those who are indoctrinated" – so in original (brackets mine).

We must strike from our path any opposition. We must use for our tools any authority that comes to hand. And then at last, the decades sped; we can dispense with all authority save our own, and triumph in the greater glory of Party.

CHAPTER XV
PROPOSALS WHICH MUST BE AVOIDED

There are certain damaging movements that could interrupt a Psychopolitical conquest. These, coming from some quarters of the country, might gain headway and should be spotted before they do, and stamped out.

Proposals may be made by large and powerful groups in the country to return the insane to the care of those who have handled mental healing for tribes and populaces for centuries - the priest. Any movements to place clergymen in charge of institutions should be fought on the grounds of incompetence and insanity brought about by religion. The most destructive thing that could happen to a Psychopolitical programme would be the investment of the ministry with the care of the nation's insane. If mental hospitals operated by religious groups are in existence, they must be discredited and closed, no matter what the cost, for it might occur that the actual figures of recovery in such institutions would become known, and that the lack of recovery in general institutions might be compared to them, and this might lead to a movement to place the clergy in charge of the insane. Every argument must be advanced early, to overcome any possibility of this ever occurring.

A country's law must carefully be made to avoid any rights of person to the insane. Any suggested laws or Constitutional amendments, which make the harming of the insane unlawful, should be fought to the extreme, on the grounds that only violent measures can succeed. If the law were to protect the insane, as it normally does not, the entire Psychopolitical programme would very possibly collapse.

Any movement to increase or place under surveillance the orders required to hospitalize the mentally ill should be discouraged. This should be left entirely in the hands of persons well under the control of Psychopolitical operatives. It should be done with minimal formality, and no recovery[156] of the insane from an institution should be possible by any process of law. Thus, any movement to add to the legal steps of the processes of commitment and release should be discouraged on the grounds of emergency. To obviate this, the best action is to place a psychiatric and detention ward for the mentally ill in every hospital in a land.[157]

Any writing of a Psychopolitical nature, accidentally disclosing themselves, should be prevented. All actual literature on the subject of insanity and its treatment should be suppressed, first by actual security, and second by complex verbiage which renders it incomprehensible. The actual figures of recovery or death should never be announced in any papers. Any investigation attempting to discover whether or not psychiatry or psychology has ever cured anyone should immediately be discouraged and laughed to scorn, and should mobilize at that point, all Psychopolitical operatives. At first, it should be ignored, but if this is not possible, the entire weight of all Psychopoliticians in the nation should be pressed into service. Any tactic possible should be employed to prevent this from occurring.

To rebut it, technical appearing papers should exist as to the tremendous number of cures effected by psychiatry and psychology, and whenever possible, percentages of cures, no matter how fictitious, should be worked into legislative papers, thus forming background of "evidence" which would immediately rebut any effort to actually

---

[156] Obviously what is meant by "recovery" is "release from" or "discharge from" mental hospitals.

[157] In great measure, the "Merchants of Chaos" has largely succeeded as Mr. Stickley had prophesied.

discover anyone who had ever been helped by psychiatry or psychology.

If the Communist connections of a Psychopolitician should become disclosed, it should be attributed to his own carelessness, and he should, himself, be immediately branded as eccentric within his own profession.

Authors of literature which seek to demonstrate the picture of a society under complete mental control and duress should be helped toward infamy or suicide to discredit their works.

Any legislation liberalizing any healing practice should be immediately fought and defeated. All healing practices should gravitate entirely to authoritative levels, and no other opinions should be admitted, as these might lead to exposure.

Movements to improve youth should be invaded and corrupted, as this might interrupt campaigns to produce in youth delinquency, addiction, drunkenness, and sexual promiscuity.

Communist workers in the field of newspapers and radio should be protected wherever possible by striking out of action, through Psychopolitics, any persons consistently attacking them. These, in their turn, should be persuaded to give every possible publicity to benefits of Psychopolitical activities under the heading of "science". No healing group devoted to the mind must be allowed to exist within the borders of Russia or its satellites. Only well-vouched-for Psychopolitical operatives can be continued in their practice and this only for the benefit of the government or against enemy prisoners.

Any effort to exclude psychiatrists or psychologist from the armed services must be fought. Any inquest into the "suicide" or sudden mental derangement of any political leader in a nation must be conducted only by Psychopolitical operatives or their dupes, whether Psychopolitics is responsible or not.

Death and violence against persons attacking Communism in a nation should be eschewed as forbidden. Violent activity against such persons might bring about their martyrdom. Defamation, and the accusation of insanity, alone should be employed, and they should be brought at last under the ministrations of Psychopolitical operatives, such as psychiatrists and controlled psychologists.

CHAPTER XVI
IN SUMMARY

In this time of unlimited weapons, and in national antagonisms where atomic war with Capitalistic powers is possible, Psychopolitics must act efficiently as never before. Any and all programmes of Psychopolitics must be increased to aid and abet the activities of other Communist agents throughout the nation in question.

The failure of Psychopolitics might well bring about the atomic bombing of the Motherland. If Psychopolitics succeeds in its mission throughout the Capitalistic nations of the world, they will never be an atomic war, for Russia will have subjugated all of her enemies.

Communism has already spread across one sixth of the inhabited world. Marxist doctrines have already penetrated the remainder. An extension of the Communist social order is everywhere victorious. The spread of Communism has never been by force of battle, but by conquest of the mind. In Psychopolitics we have refined this conquest to its last degree.

The Psychopolitical operative must succeed, for his success means a world of peace.[158] His failure might well mean the destruction of the civilized portions of Earth by atomic power in the hands of Capitalistic madmen.

The end thoroughly justifies the means. The degradation of populaces is less inhuman than their destruction by atomic fission, for to an animal that lives only once, any life is sweeter than death.

---

[158] To communists, fascists, and Islamic fundamentalists, the word "peace" has an altogether different meaning than the word has to a mainstream American. To US, "peace" is defined as the absence of war or conflict; to the afore-mentioned groups, the word "peace" means the absence of resistance to conquest.

The end of war is the control of a conquered people. If people can be conquered in the absence of war, the end of war will have been achieved without the destruction of war. A worthy goal.

The Psychopolitician has his reward in the nearly unlimited control of populaces, in the uninhibited exercise of passion,[159] and the glory of the Communist conquest over the stupidity of the enemies of the people.

{The end}

This is the end of the text written by Charles Stickley

---

[159] To a Communist, "passion" is equal to "sexual lust", and aberrations of the baser variety.

AFTERWORD
by: WebPastor David Todeschini

We see where the philosophy of Psychopolitics has led Russia. Once a superpower, the USSR is now defunct. However, their ideas are still alive and well in our society, and one cannot kill an idea by killing the people who have that idea, or by winning a war against them. After all, we defeated Germany, and we still have Nazis.[160] We annihilated Japan and they have taken over the electronics industry that we invented. We took back the Kuwait from Saddam Hussein in Desert Storm in 1991, and we have 30,000 dead soldiers from Gulf War disease. We bombed Baghdad almost into oblivion, we are using depleted uranium bullets, and we have more casualties, and an ecological disaster that will make Iraq, Afghanistan, Bosnia, Kosovo, and much of the Middle East uninhabitable for BILLIONS of years.[161] In the process, we brought terrorism to our shores. Those who are in the know, know the reasons for the terrorism being imported here. You will not hear this on the NEWS… but it is true.

The US government created this monster under Jimmy Carter, when we trained terrorists in Afghanistan. We have become the effect of a cause that we (the US) initiated. The failure to acknowledge the facts does not make the facts any less true. Denial exacerbates the problem.

We are dealing now with another form of Psychopolitics - the war waged with fear. *"… Yea, skin for skin"*, the Devil said to God in the book of Job, *"…all that a man hath, will he give for his life".*[162] In order to advance their "One World Government" agenda, it is entirely

---

[160] Not only do we have Nazis, but also we have welcomed them to live amongst us.

[161] The "half-life" of Uranium is 4-1/2 billion years. In 9 Billion years, the radioactive ordinance lying around those countries will STILL be lethally radioactive. Gulf War Disease is largely caused by the US military using this dastardly form of weapon.

[162] Job 2:4

possible that the US government allowed 9-11 to happen on purpose.[163] I include on my web site, several articles I wrote on the topic of terrorism, and include some references for you to research on your own. *"My people are destroyed for lack of knowledge"*,[164] it says in the book of Hosea. Do not be the one who parishes, because you listen and believe the NEWS media. Do your own research, and you'll will find out that the media is not only NOT informing you about what you should know, but the news media is "bought out" by the One World Government Communist agenda.

The Illuminati,[165] are alive and well in the once-great US of A., and if we don't wake up and take back our government, the next war that spans the globe, will be the one that the only the cockroaches survive. [166]

What is contained in the preceding text is important, because it thoroughly describes the mindset of those who have a "One World Government / New World Order" agenda, and are operating in the "shadows" of the apparency that appears to be a "free country" in the United States. If we fail to recognize true conspiracies for what they really are, and label those individuals who attempt to sound the alarm by presenting the available evidence, we, in this country, addicted to spectator sports, freely available psychopharmacology (legal and illegal), and enamored of instant gratification, may very well wake up one day to the sound of goose-stepping[167] in the streets.

– DT

---

[163] See: www.copvcia.com also see: www.Net4TruthUSA.com and www.RadioLiberty.com

[164] Hosea 4:6 (KJV)

[165] "Illuminati" – literally "The Illuminated Ones"

[166] It has been stated that only cockroaches and some forms of beetles will survive a global nuclear conflict that wipes our all other life forms.

[167] "Goose-Stepping" – The marching of Nazi soldiers in street parades during the reigh of Adolf Hitler.

NEW ERA MIND CONTROL

An addendum to:
A Synthesis of the Russian Textbook on Psychopolitics
© Copyright 2004 - David Todeschini - all rights reserved

INTRODUCTION

By: Dr. M.E. Tranquillo, Psy. D[168]

Over 50 years has passed since the codification in synthesis, of the Russian Textbook on Psychopolitics by American professor Charles Stickley,[169] and although the text was an accurate presentation of the policies of the Kremlin and KGB at the time, much has changed these past 50 years, and the manual is in need of an update - not that it is obsolete; the update only brings the textbook into context with the 21st Century, of which its prophesies were eerily accurate.

While the synthesis by Charles Stickley was designed to raise American awareness of the Communist agenda and methodologies in a pathetic attempt to foil them,[170] Stickley's synthesis was never widely circulated.[171] Due to both the incredulous goals, and the paucity with which the author treated the descriptions of the tactics postulated in order to bring about the Communist's goals, most of those who would have read his book, would have thought of it as more satirical than factual. As a result, those who did read it, thought it incredible, and thus would not be prepared to evaluate its true prophetic nature.

---

[168] M.E. Tranquillo is a fictitious name – David Todeschini is writing this "in his stead".

[169] Sent to the Church of Christ, Scientist and the Church of Scientology by the original author around 1955.

[170] Although eloquent in his presentation, Mr. Stickley offered no suggestions for the target audience on how to circumvent the KGB's efforts to undermine the American society.

[171] Probably because of the poor grammar (throughout) and hard-to-follow lines of reasoning.

For reasons of historical accuracy, the original text of the book is presented verbatim in the preceding pages, as the author of this addendum updates it with footnotes and short evaluations at the end of each chapter, where appropriate. While professor Stickley sought to destroy our mission, his independent chronicle of our agenda 50 years ago, serves the psychopolitical student well. Stickley examines the American society that has been shaped, molded, and transformed by our methodology, and the student who reads his analysis can only conclude that our methodology has worked - and it has worked far better than Nikita Khrushchev ever dared to dream of.

The Russian government never considered the collection of a description of all its major socio-political agendas to be published as a bound volume (or sent over a yet unforeseen Internet) for fear of being discovered by the American Dogs. However, the atmosphere has changed, and we believe that in the 21st Century, many, many more people will embrace what you will find within these pages.[172] We are standing on the edge of the greatest ideological victory ever won by man.

My assessment here in these few pages would not do justice to the great work done by your fathers and predecessors - the Alumni of Lenin University, where these concepts were first presented. In short summary, we have:

- Succeeded in promoting the religion of Darwinian Evolution in the tradition of the greatest evangelist of our cause, Thomas Huxley, whose axiom "Ontology[173] recapitulates Phylogeny",[174] is still in the American science and biology textbooks today, 130 years after it was proven to be a total fraud.[175]

---

[172] We DO have the American Communist Party; it is alive and well in the United States.

[173] "Ontology" - the roster of what there is - branches of philosophical inquiry.

[174] "Ontology recapitulates Phylogeny" - the insane idea that a human embryo goes through the four stages of Darwinian Evolution (fish, amphibian, reptile, and mammal) as it develops in vivo.

[175] Huxley was convicted of fraud in his own university (in Germany), by a jury of his peers.

- Succeeded in getting religion, the "opiate of the masses" banned from all public educational institutions.
- Succeeded in promoting rampant sexual promiscuity with its attendant abortion, drug addictions, and incurable Sexually Transmitted Diseases.
- Succeeded in ever-increasing aberrations of the tax laws,[176] with the effectual incremental abolition of private property.
- Succeeded in the enactment of gun control, and the gradual disarming of the American public.
- Succeeded in the drugging of over 9 million children in public schools on the pretense of treating fictitious maladies such as "Attention Deficit Disorder" (ADD/ADHD, et al.)
- Succeeded in driving the crime rate out-of-control, and prison populations 6 to 19 times that of any other Western nation[177] ("free country", indeed!).
- Succeeded in turning every technological advancement - particularly the computer, into a tool for the State to use in the infringement of privacy, under the guise of "National Security".

Our accomplishments are truly remarkable in light of the so-called "vigilance" of a free people. We of superior intellect, have easily and almost effortlessly, made the United States a vassal State, and even their "elite" and "cognoscenti"[178] have failed to stir from their idyllic slumber. Many years of material affluence and preoccupation with vicarious living via the idolatry of sports heroes and movie stars,[179] although not directly an objective defined in our original plans, has rendered America stupid. ("Stupid" being defined as either the love of, or the pursuit of ignorance. Surely they will perish at our whim for lack of knowledge).[180]

---

[176] The graduated income tax, and Social Security, are planks of the Communist Manifesto

[177] USDJ statistics as of 2003

[178] "Cognoscenti" – those who are cognizant; those "in the know".

[179] An inordinate number of people have committed to memory an interminable litany of useless sports trivia, and can argue for hours on end about sports, but know little of American History.

[180] Reference to the Bible – (paraphrased) Hosea 4:6 (KJV).

All this, dear Comrades, should not cause you to be complacent in your pursuits, or cause you to feel that the really important work has already been done. No, there is still much to be accomplished, and yet more territory to be taken. There remains in our path, two main enemies that we must defeat: The Christians and the Scientologists.

In the rare cases where one is a Bible-believing Christian who is also a trained Scientologist; these are most dangerous, and must be eliminated or at least neutralized by any means at your disposal. The challenge for the 21st Century is to continue to exploit the emerging technologies and psycho-pharmacology, to enable a smooth and effortless transition to a New World Order, and a single center for World Government; peace to all mankind, through the doctrine of Lenin and Marx. We can have Utopia in our lifetime.

The future is in your hands.

- M.E. Tranquillo

RELIGION

All throughout recorded human history, in the feebleness of those minds insufficiently evolved[181] to recognize the stark realities of life, man, or more precisely, the look-alike progenitors of the species *Homo Sapiens Sapiens,*[182] have resorted to the opiate of "faith" - a belief in any number of what can only be called "delusional fantasies", upon which to trust their fate, when they, themselves lose control of it. An interminable litany of such fanciful Deities has been invented, but by far, the most popular and persistent, and therefore the most threatening of these, which is diametrically opposed to our mission, is the Jesus Christ of Christianity.

The idols and polytheistic religions: Baal, Ashtoreth, Molech,[183] and the rest, have passed into obscurity, and as a result are of no consequence here. However, Christianity persists, and thus it presents a direct and viable threat to the State. Christianity's tenets put "God" above the authority of the State in the belief that *"...they are endowed by their Creator with certain inalienable rights..."* which is espoused in their Constitution and Bill of Rights.

Our operatives in the movie and toy industry, primarily, have made some inroads into the religious fabric of America, with the promotion of Ouija boards, and occult-based motion pictures and most recently, of Witchcraft. The popular TV series "Buffy"[184] mixes the sexual attraction to cute young girls (or boys) with vampirism, demons, and such-like. The "Secret Spells Barbie" dolls, and the Harry Potter movies are true Orwellian-style brainwashing at its very best. The

---

[181] Psychiatry and psychology hold that Man is a product of evolution, not creation by God.

[182] Homo Sapiens Sapiens (Latin) "The wiser wise man" or "The wise, sentient creature".

[183] Jeremiah 32:35 *"And they built the high places of Baal, which are in the valley of the son of Hinnom, to cause their sons and their daughters to pass through the fire unto Molech; which I commanded them not, neither came it into my mind, that they should do this abomination, to cause Judah to sin."*

[184] "Buffy The Vampire Slayer" – a popular TV series featuring witchcraft, spells, *et.al.*

undermining of religion in all its forms; Christianity in particular, should be top priority of any aspiring Socialist's career. Our advocates in the American Communist Lawyer's Union (ACLU) stand ready to assist the operative who can contrive any case against the teaching of religion or about God in the public schools. This has largely been accomplished. We also must remove all mention of God from the currency, the courtrooms, the TV and radio airwaves, and eventually enact the prohibition of any publication containing any sort of religion, or religious overtones.

Now, comrade, do not err in under-estimating the enemy. Although it seems that our control of the US NEWS media is all but complete; the major *coup de' tat* being the institution of the universally-viewed Communist News Network (CNN), our operative Ted Turner and his consort, "Hanoi" Jane Fonda, have totally neglected to address the issue of the Internet; that medium to which an ever-increasing number of people are turning for their NEWS coverage.

For those aspiring agents with a technical bent, this frontier must be brought under State control, possibly under some trumped-up, moralistic premise, so that the State can approve or censor what America, and ultimately, the world, has access to.

The recent child-abuse scandal within the Catholic Church was a stroke of genius; it effectively turned many Christians from their faith, and put some of the "victims" under the care of psychiatrists, who for the most part share our philosophy, if not our agenda. It is most refreshing to witness the absolute brilliance with which these anonymous comrades pulled-off this deception.

No one in the Media, who is controlled by our operatives, had asked the obvious question: *"How come you waited until now to reveal this?"* of the alleged victims. And no one <u>dared</u> to take up the defense - even of a priest - and therein was the unwitting subversion and effective undermining of perhaps the most revered of Constitutional tenets: the presumption of innocence. Hereafter, anyone entrusted with the care of children, except the State, is subject to suspicion, unfounded allegations, and if not politically-motivated malicious prosecutions, then at least the destruction of their reputations such that they are stripped of their ministry, never to be trusted again.

This tactic is so effective, that no attempt at a defense is made, and *risk management* on the part of the accused, is the only viable recourse against the mentality of a public so conditioned by the NEWS Media, who are bent towards witch-hunts instead of justice. The Catholic Church's Inquisition in eras past has engaged in such things; John Huss[185] was burned at the stake for heresy. The present mindset of the American public, to see all priests as potential sexual deviants may indeed be poetic justice. No doubt, the scandal was engineered by several of our "deep undercover" operatives, and with the NEWS Media sharing our agenda; they were all too willing to go along.

If the State is to assume control of the behavior of the masses, its authority must be ultimate and absolute; its decrees cannot be subservient to any "God" conjured up in the minds of its subjects. Those who would teach otherwise must be neutralized.

It is patently impossible to erase the religious scriptures from the face of the Earth, as we once thought possible and sought to do on so many occasions in history. Indeed, the forbidding of certain books we have found by bitter experience, only encourages even those who would otherwise have had no interest in such writings, to seek out of curiosity if nothing else, to learn why those writings have been banned.

Instead, we have found that the opposite approach, coupled with covert suggestions of low-level ridicule - just enough to cause doubt in

---

[185] An early Protestant reformist who taught "salvation is by grace alone" thus robbing the early Catholic Church of revenues gained by the selling of "indulgences".

those who have not yet been indoctrinated - will motivate an initial curiosity, which when satisfied to the point of boredom for lack of understanding, will cause people to put their Bibles up on the shelf "for show", and never open them again.

Some religions such as Christian Science, and Scientology claim to have unlocked the secrets of how the human mind operates. Dianetics has proven to be an invaluable aid to the psychopolitician when its technology for neutralizing aberrations is instead reversed and used to inflict the aberrations that work to our advantage. It is for this reason that these two religions must be vehemently and mercilessly attacked and completely discredited. What better means by which to do this, than to raise the suspicion of, or, with a certain audacity, actually bring charges of sexual abuse against their priests and ministers.

An astute psychopolitician knows that allegations alone are sufficient to the task of destroying an enemy's reputation, and thereby renders him harmless. The mindset we have engendered in the American people is that the accused is guilty upon an indictment, and that proof notwithstanding, he is still guilty. Anyone who doubts this should contact the Party's Psy-Ops division; I'm sure they can arrange for a demonstration to make you into a believer.

PSYCHIATRY AND PSYCHOLOGY

Our advances into these professions, even prior to the synthesis of the manual on Psychopolitics has been nothing short of phenomenal. For example, the Catholic Church, in a little-known pamphlet published in 1948, called psychiatry "a consecrated profession", and capitulated to what it called "evolution's unanswerable arguments" to justify its traditional doctrine of creation by God directly, into stating that *"...evolution is a process...and is simply God's method of creating."*[186] This, of course, is a testament to our expertise in prior years, in getting even the "astute and learned" men among this race of inferiors, to believe anything we want them to believe - even utter nonsense, and have them so confident of their convictions that they call it "science".

We have exceeded the loftiness of even those glorious victories, in that psychologists of all "stripes"; the credentialed Ph.D.s and the patently incompetent wannabe's, have gained an air of credibility in American society, in spite of the fact that their meddling is the cause of the moral collapse of the nation. Psychologists can be found in all government institutions - from grade schools to maximum-security prisons. Their chief method of "treatment" is to hold a person trapped in some past trauma or valence of criminal behavior, and to torture, drug, or physically mutilate the brain of a person to compel compliance, and/or drive him or her into a harmless state of apathy.

In the last 15 years, the Media has assisted in promoting the idea that every whit of human life can be made better by one pill or another. The classification of youthful exuberance that manifests itself as restlessness in the total absence of intellectual stimulus as "Attention Deficit Disorder" (ADD/AHDD) is a brilliant invention of modern

---

[186] This statement is absolutely true - DJT

psychiatry.[187] This brainwashing of the American public, and indeed, the world, has enabled our operatives to categorize normal human behaviors such as the "fidgeting" of a bored, gifted child, as a "mental disorder". Thus, it follows that "treatment" must ensue, and the child be prescribed various and sundry psychotropic medications which enable the Operative to more easily manipulate the mentality of his / her charges.

Operatives in the US government have assisted with the support of legislation that subsidies studies of non-existent diseases, 347 of which have been codified into the DSM-IV - the diagnosis of such, which is entirely arbitrary and a mater of opinion. The statistics are testimony to the efficacy of this propaganda. America is literally being driven insane; a major portion of the population, especially young children - 9 million as of this writing[188] - are either physically or psychologically addicted to legal psychotropic pharmacology, the production, price, and distribution of which is directly controlled by the State. The majority of parents, who perceive docility in their children as a "cure" for "hyperactivity", sing the praises of Ritalin™, Prozak™ or Adderall™ to the tune of cash register bells ringing in the coffers of several Pharmaceutical giants, which are (also) under State supervision. A more complete case of brainwashing is difficult to imagine; and of course, this did not happen by accident; such victories are seldom the work of one man, but can only be accomplished by the concerted effort of many loyal comrades, who adhere to the Marxist/Leninist philosophy, and who dare to commit the outrageous in the teeth of the phantom that has been called "reason". A big lie is believable, because the effort to dissect it and see it for what it is… is beyond the mental ability of most Americans. They will accept the word of a "credentialed expert", because they lack the mental ability to reason for themselves.

---

[187] Attention Deficit / Hyperactivity is a fictitious disease with no basis in fact, whatsoever. For further information, see: www.cchr.org or www.freedommag.org and links from www.Net4TruthUSA.com/CCHRLinks.htm

[188] November 2004.

However, dear comrades, again, do not be deceived into thinking that such an easy victory will maintain itself well a continuous effort on our part. If any axiom of the constitutional Republic is true, none is truer than the admonition about constant vigilance. America fail to maintain its vigilance and their Republic is about to crumble in our fists. We must take heed to be vigilant, especially towards the only two remaining threats: Christianity and Scientology. Both of these religions are concerned primarily with the soul or Thetan (respectively); and while the former relies primarily on faith to instill belief in its parishioners, the latter has, since 1951 or so, claimed to have proven the existence of this soul by scientific methodology.

Scientology arose out of Dianetics, which is a science that is the polar opposite of psychology. Other organizations such as Citizens Commission on Human Rights (CCHR) and Freedom Magazine have engaged in numerous campaigns to destroy the marvelous achievement of the Party over the past 50 years. It is imperative that the psychopolitical operative avoid detection by the groups associated with Scientology; Christians who are unfamiliar with our tactics, are easily lead down fruitless "rabbit trails" if they discover our subversions. Scientologists, however, are not so easily deceived. They have been responsible for the closing of many of our model asylums, and instrumental in the criminal prosecution of many of our agents and operatives.

A central technical Center "PSYTAC" has been organized in the Kremlin, in order to deal specifically with Scientology. Operatives at PSYTAC have been handpicked from among the best psychoterrorists, trained in black Dianetics, and organized into a worldwide network. Their mission is covert tactical support for any PSYOPS member, or unwitting dupe who has stumbled into enemy hands, or fallen under Scientological[189] scrutiny. The operative need not contact PSYTAC, the organization has at its disposal, all of the

---

[189] "Scientological" – having to do with Scientology (or Dianetics).

necessary communications and intelligence from FieldOps, to be instantly advised when any operative, agent, or dupe requires assistance. You need not worry comrade; Big Brother is watching.

Technology and Control

Our efforts to usurp modern technology to the task of micro-management of every sentient being on the planet have been glorious triumphs these last 30 years, in particular.

In the 1970s, the American Company IBM developed what it called the Universal Product Code (UPC). This barcode, readable by scanning laser, can be seen on every product sold in America. Most retail stores have automated their inventories with the bundled software, and thus are reluctant to carry products without this barcode on the package. The developer used the number six as a synchronization character, which is represented by two narrow vertical lines at the beginning, middle and end of the barcode. Early (circa 1970-71) products had these lines labeled with corresponding numbers, and Christians were quick to notice that "666" (the mark of the beast of Revelation Chapter 13) was common to all UPC codes. Subsequently the lines (bars) were not labeled, but the "666" is still there. Modern technology has developed an implantable[190] microchip that can also be scanned with this "point of sale" technology.

It is now possible to keep track of every retail transaction, no matter how small, and with the mandatory implantation of these ID chips into people, we will be able to know and to control every single transaction-down to the purchase of cigarettes or bubble gum. Several banks have released credit cards with these ID chips in them. They are marketed as a "convenience"; *i.e.:* you can "Blink"™ your purchases without waiting online. The logical evolution of this technology is to keep track of the person's whereabouts by miniature "Blink"™ card sensors in key locations in a city. The New York subway system is, as of this writing (Jan. 2006), testing such a chip to be carried on a keychain, designed to replace its Metro-card.™ In the future, those who are not loyal Party members will be denied all transaction and

---

[190] "Implantable" – ability to be implanted.

travel privileges. Our operatives have incorporated a company devoted to the development of this technology. The company name is MONDEX (from: **Mon**etary = money, and **Dex**ter = pertaining to the right hand). MasterCard, Inc., immediately acquired a 51% share of the Company.[191]

The only missing ingredient is the personal ID chips which must be implanted into citizens, and there is a plan being formulated by our PsyOps team, which will shortly under the guise of national security in the wake of another 9-11 type incident, that will have most Americans lining up to get these implants just as they lined up like cattle during-the-post-depression years, to get their Social Security numbers. Upon the Implementation of transaction / purchase control (TPC), those who do not have their chip IDs will be unable to consummate any legal transactions. Reduced to a barter system among those who can freely buy those who were initially reluctant to be implanted with ID chips, will submit to the procedure or starve.

Our test In October 2003, of a mobile ElectroMagnetic Pulse (EMP) device, mounted in a specially outfitted Econoline[192] van, was also a great success. TekOps[193] "Operation Candlelight", used this EMP device - simply a very large Tesla coil[194] - a very high-voltage transformer - to inject a sharp "ringing" pulse electricity into the Niagara Mohawk power grid. Electronic load monitoring computers all along the grid network sensed the fluctuation on the lines, and automatically opened switches to isolate the apparent fault. Of course, suddenly disconnecting hundreds of thousands of Amps of load, caused additional line spikes and disturbances, and within minutes, a major part of the East Coast was burning candles in the dark.

---

[191] This statement is absolutely true.

[192] "Econoline" – a model (series) of panel vans.

[193] "TekOps" – Technical Operations.

[194] Tesla Coil – a large, high-voltage coil that is used to convert low voltage AC current into extremely high voltages – on the order of millions of volts. (see local Library or Internet for : Nikola Tesla for complete history)

The Canadian power companies were quick to point to Niagara Falls as the point of impact. They announced "a possible lightning strike", which really wasn't far from the truth. However, FEMA officials were quick to recognize this as an act of terrorism. In order to avoid embarrassment in the wake of 9-11, quickly conspired with the Media, and contrived the totally incredulous lie that the problem was caused by utility workers in Ohio who accidentally cut into a local power line while trimming branches off a tree. The big lie was believed without question by the public, as our comrades in the media presented as established fact. Of course, this is not the first time we have pulled off such an incredible deception.

The cover-up we did with TWA Flight 800 was probably the best example of Media-Control prior to September 11, 2001, and right "up there" with the cover-ups of the JFK assassination, the WTC bombing in '93, Waco, Ruby Ridge, and Oklahoma City. The graduates of our psychopoilitical colleges have surely made fools of the American people, and have the "elite" under their thumb.

The example set by Operation Candlelight is perhaps the best illustration of late, which demonstrates the utter truth in the axiom which states: "If you tell a lie often, long, and loud enough, people will believe it"; and its corollary "A big lie is believed without question". This axiom is the foundation of Psychopolitics. Anyone who has ever tested it in the laboratory of the real world has never been disappointed with its efficacy; its effects are almost miraculous, and certainly magical. It can be depended upon even more so than the laws of physics. The psychopolitician need not question it, or hesitate to use it.

BIOLOGY

Our scientists, working incognito, and outside the jurisdiction of the international science communities, have developed a variety of biotoxins, and had supplied culture samples to Iraq prior to the 1991 Gulf War. As a result, over 30,000 delayed casualties among American troops have been sustained, and these "Once Warriors" have taken these contagious diseases back home with them.[195] Our operatives in the US Veterans Administration have ensured that the cover-ups and misdiagnoses[196] continue, until the epidemic can run its full course. Certain miscalculations concerning the other pathogens have been corrected for the current deployment. The improved pathogens are undetectable, genetically engineered retroviruses similar to SIV/HIV and Ebola. The effects will not be known for years - at least until 2013.

Other Bio weapons projects are being conducted, and due to the extremely sensitive nature of these missions, discussion in detail outside the scope of the project supervisor, is prohibited under penalty of death. The KGB has full responsibility to oversee BioLab[197] projects. If you are an operative with related training, or know a dupe who would be interested in Bio weapons development, contact your coordinator.

DRUG MARKETS

We have a network of operatives who deal exclusively in the illegal drug trade. We've known for decades, that the CIA funds many of its operations out of drug profits. We have assisted the CIA with numerous high-level drug deals, and continue to do so. The growing drug culture in America creates a dampening of resistance to our

---

[195] See the "Ill Wind" issue of Freedom Magazine available free on www.freedommag.org
[196] "Desert Storm" veterans who went to the VA hospitals and presented symptoms of "Gulf War Illness" were told that "It's all in your head" and sent to psychiatrists who prescribed mind-altering drugs.
[197] "BioLab" – Biological Laboratory.

propaganda. Minds which are preoccupied with obtaining illegal drugs cannot offer any resistance, and those young children raised on Ritalin™ and taught Darwinian Evolution, do not ever develop the self-esteem, nor a knowledge of their "inalienable rights", or of a Creator (God), and so do not even attempt to resist.

The Twin-tined pitchfork of illegal drugs and prescribed legal psychopharmacology is also a medium by which the Party is able to fund extravagant and highly complex psychoterrorism projects, which are vital to the attainment of One World Government and a New World Order within the next 20 years. The users currently addicted to illegal drugs are our slaves. The drugs would not be available if we did not permit it, and when we withdraw our cooperation, every single heroin and crack cocaine addict will do whatever we tell them to do, for their next "hit".

THE LEGAL SYSTEM

A visit to any prison law library would convince the most critical skeptic, that justice is a mere illusion in the United States these days. The Party owes its profound gratitude to the ACLU - the American Communist Lawyer's Union, and the Masonic Lodge, for American Jurisprudence; undoubtedly the most confusing and wholly exasperating tangle of contradictions in the whole of human history.

In New York, for example, the lowest county courts are called "Supreme Court", and the highest State courts are called "Court of Appeal". On the federal level, the district courts often vary widely - even to the extent of being exactly the polar opposites in their opinions and rulings.

Prior to the mid-1980s, prisoners were more evenly matched to their adversarial prosecutors, as both had access to the exact same tools

- printed volumes and manual typewriters. With the advent of computer technology, prosecutors can search online databases in a matter of seconds, which puts prisoners at a distinct disadvantage.

A prisoner without access to these tools and online services, can spend months manually searching for the same case law, and never find it. Most prisoners are also functionally illiterate. Legal assistance is from inmate paralegals that know little of the law. The last great legend among jailhouse lawyers - "Jerry the Jew" has long since been out-of-action. He is on a respirator[198] in a hospital bed at Wende prison[199] in Alden, New York. "Justice" is a joke in the United States, and fodder for comedy skits on Saturday Night Live. If anyone could understand it, it would be the ultimate "gut-buster".

This is goodness for the Party, since the court system as corrupt as it is, maintains the apparency of due process. The inability of most prisoners to file successful *pro se'* appeals of their cases, - the level at which the public perceives it - makes the system seem to be infallible. In this case, the Orwellian axiom that "Bad is good" fitly applies. Lies a look like truth, and truth, which denies the lies, can be manipulated by any novice psychopolitician, into that great "cubbyhole" / buzzword invented by our comrades in the PsyOps[200] division: *"Denial"*.

PRISON REHABILITATION

Nothing is a more versatile instrument in the hands of a Merchant of Chaos, than a prison population that can be driven to an escalating cycle of criminal activity and historically unprecedented levels of recidivism. The advantages to the psychopolitician are numerous. Among the major benefits to the goals of the Party are:

---

[198] As of when this section was written – April 2004.
[199] Wende Correctional Facility is a maximum-security prison near Buffalo, New York.
[200] "PsyOps" – Psychological Operations.

An increased crime rate (real or perceived) is the only excuse a psychopolitician needs to rally support for tougher laws, which in turn, directly causes more crime and higher recidivism, as we shall explain shortly.

Provides the mandate and the funding for close monitoring of individuals post-incarceration, and State jobs for parole officers, psychiatrists, psychologists, and other *Hick Farmer Sigmund Freud Wannabes*, Party sympathizers, and unwitting dupes.

Provides a population based upon which PsyOps can conduct psychological and psycho pharmaceutical experiments, largely without monitoring or supervision by "human rights" organizations.

Biosystems[201] can have an isolated (quarantined) population on which to test experimental Bio-weapons and vaccines.

Prison populations are tallied in the census for the host County or town, and thus provide an artificial means for raising Federal funds for that town, thus giving the psychopolitician the advantage of the vote in his district, when he supports a building or expanding of prisons.[202]

MANIPULATING RECIDIVISM

We owe a debt of gratitude to our humanitarian nemesis, the late L. Ron Hubbard, who developed the science of Dianetics. Prior to the codification of this technology, it was generally suspected, but in-exactly known, by what methodology a criminal could be created from a non-criminal or a true criminal to be rehabilitated into a model citizen.

---

201 "Biosystems" – Biological Systems – the Russian research group researching biology.
202 This statement is absolutely true.

Up until our scientists got hold of Dianetics, and most importantly Mr. Hubbard's book "Fundamentals of Thought", the mechanism which caused aberrant behavior was explained only by a jumble of incomprehensible dissertations in the field of criminology. Upon the unveiling of Dianetics technology, this nebulous mechanism was elegantly and clearly explained as "asserted rightness". Our PsyOps division has experimented with this mechanism, and has found it to operate precisely as Mr. Hubbard described. Basically:

A person who has violated his own ethics will tend to justify the behavior (or crime), because he's trying to "do good". He cannot undo his Overt act (or crime), and he computes that if he could be "right" (i.e.: justified), he could resolve the conflict with his conscience (or superego) which psychiatry calls "dissonance". And so actual "rightness" (good) quickly becomes separated from his assertion of rightness, and he then will repeat the offense in order to maintain his assertion that the behavior was "good". This is perhaps an incomplete and cursory explanation here; however, let me assure you that understanding this mechanism and reversing it; using it to using it to aberrate an individual, creates the most predictable spin into criminal insanity imaginable. Details of the precise method of application being beyond the scope and the purpose of this tome. Suffice it to say that both the withholding of the concept of absolute forgiveness for sins (as in Christianity), and holding the person in the valence of his past criminal behavior[203] by continually reminding him of how wrong he was, keeping "rap sheets" on file forever, etc. is virtually a 100% guarantee of creating a "career criminal".

This precise methodology, although uncodified for security reasons, is the basis for almost every State-run prison "rehab" program in the country. The notable exceptions are programs run by *Prison Fellowship Ministries, Kairos*[204] *Prison Ministries, Residents Encounter Christ*, all Christian organizations, and the *Criminon*™, and

---

[203] This is the opposite practice of Dianetics, which discovers the valence and resolves it.
[204] Kairos is a Greek word meaning "The Lord's Good Time".

Narconon™ programs sponsored by the Church of Scientology. These programs are almost 100% effective in the rehabilitation of former criminals.

Note: see December 2003 issue of Mother Jones Magazine, on: www.motherjones.com an article entitled "Jesus Goes to Jail". Also see:
www.criminon.org and www.narconon.org

If the Party is to maintain its base of incorrigible criminals as status quo, we cannot afford the introduction of any efficable rehabilitation programs into the prisons. The fear of crime is too valuable a tool for the psychopolitician to lose. Only by engineering exponential increases in violent crime can the Party have a valid mandate for the future declaration of martial law, and implementation of the Police State that is consistent with our future goals.

THE GOAL of the GAOL[205]

The mission of any psychopolitician in a position of influence within the prison system is to ensure that only psychology based "rehab" programs are available, and preferably those which employ Black Dianetics as previously described. Insofar as it is possible within the constraints of still existing prisoner's rights legislation, access to all Christian-based programs such as Prison Fellowship, Kairos, Residents Encounter Christ, Alternative to Violence Project, and the Scientology programs Criminon and Narconon, should be eliminated, severely restricted, or made to be as difficult-to-conduct as possible.

A psychopolitician in charge of a prison, can always arrange an "incident" within these programs, and then cite prison security concerns if the restrictive policy is challenged in court. The courts will

---

[205] Gaol – archaic word for "prison" or "jail"

always uphold even ridiculous policies that a prison administration can fabricate to create a credible apparency of "reasonable cause" to restrict such activities based on security concerns.

PSYCHOTERRORISM

The term "psychoterrorism" may be relatively new, but in point-of-fact, the methodology is nothing new. As recently as World War II, Adolph Hitler used his SS troops to set fire to the Reichstag (German Parliament building), then blamed the Gypsies and the Jews for "acts of terrorism" to get himself elected as dictator. The CIA staged the Gulf of Tonkin incident in order to have an excuse to get into the Vietnam conflict, the "threat" of Bio nuclear W.M.D.s was an excuse for the latest attack on Iraq. Prior to this, there is no doubt that 9-11 was a PsyOps plot to terrify the American people into trading their civil liberties for a false sense of security. This writer, is not privy to every psychopolitical operation, but I can assure the reader that September 11th was masterfully engineered with the tacit, if not full consent of US government officials; Party operatives who served the cause well.

At present (November 2004), we have engineered a virtual Nazi Police State in America. As of October 2001, with the passing of the USA Patriot Act, anyone can be arrested without probable cause or the protection of judicial review, and held without bail and without an attorney indefinitely. This effectively bypasses the U.S. Constitution in its entirety, as all other "guarantees" are of no effect in the absence of liberty.

The Hegelian Dialectic
How Thought is Manipulated

One of the most important concepts of Brainwashing or Thought Control to understand is the concept of Hegelian Dialectics. Basically, this technique enables the operator / agent to manipulate the thoughts of his or her victims, and get people to come to their own conclusions, which are in line with the psychopolitical agent's agenda. The end result of the dialectic process is that the psychopolitical operative gains not only cooperation from the public who are being manipulated, but also appears as the "savior" of the society. The Dialectic consists of three parts:

- PART 1:   THESIS – Which is a condition or a problem which is created for the purpose of establishing a threat.
- PART 2:   ANTITHESIS – The opposing viewpoint which will be perceived as a radical solution to the fabricated problem.
- PART 3:   SYNTHESIS – The "solution" or agenda, which is a compromise designed to implement the hidden agenda.

In the Dialectic, the SYNTHESIS is actually the goal or the agenda of the psychopolitical operator. In order to achieve that goal, which is usually accomplished over a long period of time, the psychopolitical operator sets up the thesis and an antithesis, and manipulates one against the other. The public perceives one as a threat, and the other as an unacceptable radical solution to the fabricated problem.

The compromise, or synthesis (which is actually the goal from the outset) is then presented as an amicable solution. This is best explained with the use of several (actual) examples:

Suppose that the psychopolitician wishes to control all of the firearms in a country. In order to do this, a thesis and antithesis must be set up in order to establish the problem and a radical proposition or postulated solution. One could set up a thesis that states, "There is a drug / gun / violence problem". We begin by fomenting a wave of violence in the nation's youth by the introduction of highly addictive drugs and a "gangsta" culture that glamorizes the violent lifestyle. As an antithesis, one sets up a movement that advocates the possession of weapons by the general public, as a deterrent and a defense against the violence. These conditions are both intolerable; we cannot live with violent drug addicts, and we cannot tolerate vigilantism that would result from ubiquitous gun toting in the streets. Never mind that the "right to bear arms" is guaranteed under the second amendment; that argument is easily defused by stating simply, "You don't need an M-16 to go duck hunting". Never mind that the purpose of the Founders was not to guarantee an ample supply of ducks, but the public never questions that which is stated as if it is a matter of fact. Enter the psychopolitician, who proposes various "gun control" legislation against the weapons, as if the weapons could act on their own volition. The result is the synthesis that the weapons are mostly all accounted for, and in the hands of "law-abiding" citizens (the criminal element accounts for only a small fraction of "gun owners"). The weapons can then, upon imposition of "emergency measures", be outlawed and collected at will.

Another example is that a company (in this case, DuPont) wishes to retain its monopoly on refrigerants (Freon™).[206] A synthesis is established where the chemical is made into a threat – it "depletes the ozone layer" (of course, this is total nonsense).[207] The antithesis is that we either give up our refrigerants (and aerosol propellants), or control the release of the chemical, so that it doesn't get into the atmosphere.

Controlling the release of Freon™ is prohibitively expensive – many refrigerant companies invested many thousands of dollars in equipment, training, and licensing, and some went broke. And so a phase-out of Freon™ was done, and it has been replaced by a similar chemical with a brand new patent. The synthesis or goal, which was to

---

[206] DuPont's 50-year patent on Freon™ expired in the early 1990s, which would have enabled other companies to manufacture the refrigerant without paying royalties to DuPont.

[207] Various programs in the archives of Radio Liberty at www.RadioLiberty.com establish that CFCs are not a threat to the ozone layer, and do not contribute to "global warming", which is another Hegelian Dialectic, and a hoax which has no basis in scientific fact whatsoever.

(effectively) renew the patent was accomplished, and thereby DuPont indirectly controls all the perishable food on planet Earth because without refrigerants,[208] most of the food we eat would spoil, or never reach its destination. Thereby, DuPont, can at will, create a world wide famine by simply ceasing to manufacture refrigerants.

Another agenda that has lent itself well to the dialectic process, is the slow implementation of a system of computer databases to actually track the whereabouts of human beings in preparation for the Biblical "Mark of the Beast" foretold by the Apostle Paul almost 2,000 years ago in the book of Revelation.[209] Under this system, no one can buy or sell without a "mark" (subcutaneously implanted RFID[210] chip). The thesis is presented on two fronts: Keeping track of domestic animals and livestock, and tracking criminals (sexual predators). The thesis is both a convenience and a threat, and the antithesis is loss of animals and crime out of control, respectively.

In this scenario, these chips (called "Digital Angel") are inexpensive, and provide for the installation of nation-wide computer systems and interconnected databases in order to make the synthesis work. We will never lose another domestic pet, or lose track of ex-convicts (who, they tell us) are likely to commit more crimes against helpless women and children. The synthesis is instantly accepted. Once the equipment is installed, and the databases interconnected, it will be another thesis / antithesis with its attendant synthesis which authorizes the "registration" of every person in the United States. Once the equipment and the digital infrastructure is in place, it is easy to add data for all citizens into the database. We see this dialectic being implemented in numerous forms from the "EZ-Pass"™ toll system, to the Chase "Blink"™ credit cards with built in RFID chips.

---

[208] When equipment fails, it must be replaced with equipment that uses the "new" refrigerants.
[209] See: Revelation 13:16, 17
[210] RFID – Radio Frequency Identification.

In the future, these passive chips, which require an input of energy from an external scanner device to operate, will derive their operating current from the body itself, and become active transmitters which can send a person's physical location (with the use of GPS[211] technology) from anywhere on the planet. George Orwell was a prophet.

The dialectic is accepted by the public, because they are made to believe that the synthesis is a solution to a problem, or a convenience they can no longer do without. The American and Western European societies have become increasingly dependant on a technology infrastructure, which is becoming increasingly complex, and technologically fragile. For example, if all of the Personal Computers in the US were suddenly rendered inoperative, there is no doubt that American society would suffer irreparable damage, and could possibly collapse.

The Psychopolitician's agenda is that of control. Nothing is more satisfying to the operative than to set the dialectic in motion, and observe that it works each and every time without fail.

---

[211] GPS – Global Positioning System – a system of orbiting satellites used for navigation purposes.

ARMS (gun) CONTROL

Over many, many years, Party operatives have succeeded in the diversion of the debate on the Second Amendment away from the true reason it was written into the Constitution. An astute Party member would have long ago read The Federalist Papers, wherein is explained the reasoning employed by the founders as to why certain provisions of Constitutional law came about.

The founders, cognizant of the fact that laws protecting the liberties of a nation could slowly be eroded and undermined, amended the right to bear arms to the Constitution. By an ingenious program of media propaganda, Party agents and psychopoliticians have succeeded in diverting the debate on to a discussion about which type of weapon is reasonably suited for game hunting purposes. The end-all of this diverted debate resulted in the Brady Bill, which bans the private ownership of automatic weapons. The dumbed-down[212] American public, raised on revisionist history, and distracted by a virulent addiction to spectator sports, is not concerned that the reason the founders wrote the Second Amendment was not to guarantee future generations the ability to go duck hunting. **The reason for the Second Amendment was so that citizens could protect themselves from the tyranny of their own government, should the other protections of law fail.**

EDUCATION

The Party's accomplishments in undermining American schools have been nothing short of phenomenal. Under the 10th amendment of the U.S. Constitution things that are not specified in the Constitution, are left to the individual States. Therefore the National Education Association (NEA), the Public Broadcasting System (PBS), the

---

[212] "Dumb-down" – the process of making exams in school easier so that students appear to be smarter.

National Endowment for the Arts, and all of the Federal education programs, have no basis in law to exist. But they do exist! This is testimony to the fact that the American public has become so dependent on the government, that their lives would collapse around them were it not for government "assistance".

The Party has no need outside of itself, for masses of cognoscenti who will inevitably assert their individuality above Party objectives. As covered earlier, the introduction of psychology and psychotropic drugs into the school system is a vital and indispensable tool for the control of the masses, as well as a windfall source of Federal funding via profits on these drugs that financed numerous other Party projects nationwide. The psychopolitician is encouraged to devise means by which these programs can be expanded.

The best example of how much our methodologies and nosology has influenced the field of Education, is the following little-known quote:

"Schools will become clinics whose purpose is to provide individualized psycho-social treatment for the student, and teachers must become psycho-social therapists. This will include bio-chemical and psychological mediation of learning, as drugs are introduced experimentally to improve in the learner such qualities as personality, concentration, and memory. Children are to become the objects of experimentation."

- NEA report on "Education in the '70's" [213]

At this writing (2006), there are over twenty million school-age children in the United States that are being medicated with psycho-

---

[213] Source: "The Unseen Hand" - Ralph Epperson ISBN # 0-9614135-06 - Id at 383

active drugs to "treat" the non-existent "disorders" that our operatives have created over the last 30 years.

PENAL LAW LEGISLATION

If any lesson the American people should have learned in the Prohibition years, it is this: Outlawing what people are wont to do, will not stop people from doing it, and will create a state of war, with the "outlaws" asserting their "rights" by increasing violence in civil unrest.

The Party's position on individual morality is best explained by Kohlberg's[214] "post-modernist" or "post-conventional" theory of moral development: each person is his own moral agent, and with the education provided via "outcome-based" curriculums, we can determine the outcome via the data that the organism is exposed to.

In civil law, it has for many years been known within the Party "think tanks" that harsh laws and penalties create evermore ruthless and dangerous criminals both prior to, and especially after their incarceration. Our expert propagandists in the media have succeeded in convincing the American people that the exact opposite is true; i.e.: that increasing crime requires increasingly harsher laws and penalties.[215]

It is a true datum that an astute community can drastically reduce its crime problem, and live without violence and outlaws. In order for this to happen, the entire community of "law-abiding" citizens must reach out to the errants in their midst in the spirit of Christian love and compassion. They must allow the "outcasts" to contribute to the goals of the community by whatever means they devise, without coercion. This is a most unlikely thing to have happen in today's society with several notable exceptions: Most threatening to the Party's

---

[214] Kohlberg is a "New Age" behavioral psychologist or something.
[215] This is another example of a Hegelian Dialectic.

goals are Christian "revivals", and Scientology's "Way to Happiness" projects. The Party operative should seek to sabotage such efforts, and to discredit and defame such endeavors within his or her sphere of influence.

A HOLISTIC APPROACH

It may seem overwhelming to a novice Party operative, to study and understand the many facets and nuances of the Socialist jewel. Not to worry; the novice need only devote himself to the Party philosophy, and the "what-to-do" in order to aid the cause, will follow naturally. Man's nature is to be socialistic; man, you see, is naturally a social animal. Once divested of any inclination towards individuality- a concept conceived in the minds of the Federalists - men gravitate naturally, and of their own volition, toward dependence on the State, which is in reality, and inevitably, the final authority.

Our battle has not been against Democracy, but instead against the original Constitutional Republic. Many Americans have no concept of the difference between a Republic and a Democracy. If the student here wishes to satisfy a superior intellect, he would be wise to study this. Every "Democracy" in recorded history has become a totalitarian Police State; America will not be the exception to the rule. The passage of time will bear out the truth of that statement.

All that is required to change a Republic into a Democracy is to use the courts to undermine any notion of an absolute ethical or moral authority (such as God or religion) which exalts itself over the mandates of the State. We have begun the process in earnest by legislation that permits the practice of what is forbidden by individual ethics and Scriptural law.

With the removal of God, we take away the spiritual consequences of sin. By decriminalization, we removed the civil penalties and the social stigma of cold-blooded infanticide. Via abortion-on-demand we accomplish the promotion of sexual promiscuity, and assert that axiom of psychiatry which states "Man is an animal; there is no soul", destroy the fabric of marriage and family. Consequently, the individual seeks a unity with the State in the Party, practically from his infancy. Thus we create "The International Child of the Future", and a desire to be united with the rest of humanity in a global family under a single government, and a New World Order.

The aspiring operative can clearly see the accomplishments of the Party towards this laudable goal, which is now, presently within our grasp. We at Lenin University have spared no effort or expense, and have left no pillar of the American Constitution unallied.[216] Our approach is calculated, precisely contrived, and flawlessly executed on every ideological, educational, political, legal, moralistic, religious, scientific, and psychological frontier. No stone is left unturned, and the foundations of American Imperialism are about to crumble and fall like the Twin Towers collapsed of their own weight on September 11th, 2001.

PSYCHOPOLI**TIT**IANS

The reader may have noticed the word "politician" misspelled in the title here. I assure the reader that it is no error. It is done to remind a student that his or her effectiveness is tied directly to the ample and yielding breasts ('tit' -sic) of the Federal government of the United States. For some unknown reason - possibly unresolved guilt over Hiroshima and Nagasaki, slavery, or perhaps the usurping of the Native Americans, the USA has traditionally nursed its enemies and has raised its future enemies from infancy. The psychopolitician should have no qualms or objections to being a suckling at the teats of a puppet Democracy; the "mother" will blindly nurture any suckling

---

[216] "Unassailed" – the state of NOT being under attack.

without objection. Draw as much "milk" from the system as you possibly can.

THE ROAD TO PEACE

It is to every Psychopolitician's advantage, if he or she is in the public eye, to liberally incorporate the buzzword "Peace" into every utterance that is subject to being quoted by the mass media. The reason for this is quite simple: Americans are presently, especially post 9-11, in a state of trauma and dissonance, and as a result are all too eager to support anything that promises this elusive "peace".

This may seem strange to an operative that has been raised in Soviet society, and requires clarification: You see, the Party's definition of "peace" differs from what Americans define as "peace". The American (Western) concept of peace has to do with the absence of war or violent conflicts; to the Western world, "peace" is a state of (at least) domestic tranquility. On the other hand, the Socialist's Party definition of "peace" has always been "Peace is the absence of resistance to Communism". Therefore, it can be truly said, as long as any bastion of Americanism and Western European culture remains on the planet, there will never exist a condition of "peace" as the Party has correctly defined it.

WEAPONS of MASS DISTRACTION

The Party's most effective weapon is its ability to control the media networks. The party controls the media, either directly by ownership (CNN), or vicariously by Party operatives and sympathetic dupes within it. The Party's mind-control technologies distract and refocus America's attention from the vital issues of national and global politics, onto sensationalist non-issues. Examples are the countless contrived sex scandals of late, spectator sports, or murder trials of famous celebrities such as O.J. Simpson, child abductions, more sex scandals, Michael Jackson, "Never-Land", Janet Jackson's famous Super Bowl "wardrobe malfunction", *ad nauseum*. Whatever mindless fodder can be employed to displace coverage of Party agendas, operations, and incidents, that would alert Americans to our covert operations, benefits the goals of the Party.

As the American public discovers the Internet as an alternative source of NEWS information our traditional avenues of control of information will erode, if an alternative method which is suitable to the technology is not quickly found or invented. TechOps[217] is in need of technical and legally astute personnel to brainstorm an appropriate and viable solution to this problem. If our ability to brainwash the American public by the selective availability of NEWS were in any way diminished, the attainment of our goals within the projected timeframe, would be seriously jeopardized.

ENVIRONMENTALISM

The general public is wholly ignorant of the fact that with the exception of unleashing nuclear war, mankind is utterly and completely incapable of affecting "the environment" in any lasting or significant manner. A seemingly rational argument would be the citing of England's former smog and pollution of the air over major cities such as London. What is not stated in these arguments is that these situations are highly localized and also temporary. The eruption of Mount St. Helens volcano - a relatively minor event among volcanic eruptions - poured much more pollutants into the environment in one incident, than mankind has in the whole of human history. Nature is fully capable of neutralizing the effect of man-made pollutants with the exception of radioactive wastes.

The general public is entirely ignorant of these facts, and Party operatives feigning concern over "the environment" have exploited that ignorance. These operatives have recruited from among the ignorant with nothing better to do, hordes of followers who have transformed

---

[217] "TechOps" – Technical Operations.

this concern into a veritable religion. Continued control of such organizations as Greenpeace, is vital to the Party goals.

The banning of the insecticide DDT worldwide has had little if any positive environmental impact. However, the ban was followed by an exponential increase in the mosquito population in Third World countries, which dramatically increased the incidence of malaria. The Party had contrived and used the ban on DDT as a "natural" means of population control.

The banning of the CFC (ChloroFluoroCarbons) refrigerant Freon™ coincided with the expiration of DuPont Chemical's nonrenewable worldwide patent. Had the ban not been passed, the company would have lost exclusive rights of manufacture. More importantly, the ban enabled the government to seize control of the refrigerant chemical industry.
The entire food production and distribution chain depends on refrigeration. The government that can control the production and sale of refrigerants can, at its whim, cause the almost total collapse of the food supply of all the developed (technological) nations. The Party, via its operatives, now has control of this resource.

Laws have been passed that permit government seizure of "private land" for infractions of any of the hundreds of laws pertaining to air pollution, water usage, or land erosion, mining, digging, or cultivating. Along with progressive property taxes, the environmental laws will eventually bring about an end to the private or corporate ownership of land.

CRIMINAL YOUTH

It is well known within Party research groups that the drugs currently being distributed to schoolchildren are directly responsible for exponential increases in violence, due to the simultaneous lowering of natural inhibitions, and the confusion of sensory data, which causes the ensuing dementia.

A single violent incident concerning any single individual, must immediately be blamed on a "pre-existing" mental illness, and the dosage of the drugs the patient is taking, are to be immediately increased. This course of action serves to effectively remove the suspicion of cause from the drug. This is routine sleight-of-hand for the novice psychoterrorist.

The goal of the Socialist State with regards to children, is for the State to raise them from infancy in controlled and monitored group environments separated into three categories: **1.** Infant/toddler, **2.** Preadolescent / teen, **3.** Young adult. The settings would encourage maximum conformity, and provide a large base of individuals to select from, for Neo-Eugenics and genetic engineering of future generations, and creates the ability to cull the inferior and naturally rebellious, or the intellectually deficient from the global gene pool.

In order to get parents to part with their children voluntarily, we must work to make the up-coming generations so unruly, so misbehaved, so violent, and so unmanageable, that their parents seek help from social workers, psychologists, or psychiatrists. These Party Operatives would then "diagnose" the child, and refer him or her to a State institution for treatment; a commitment which would thereafter, never be rescinded.

America's "subculture" of urban "Gangsta' Rappers" arose on its own, as a byproduct, not a design of Psychopolitics. This criminal element, comprised mostly of the inferior races, is not the gene pool material one would choose for Neo-eugenics. However this "culture" is spreading by contamination, to the rest of the more desirable portions of the society, and it is from this population that we can legally seize our initial subjects via court proceedings. For this reason, the loyal psychopolitician will support legislation that prosecutes children - at increasingly young ages - as adults. Conviction results in the subsequent incarceration in "youth homes" or "kiddy jails", whereby they can be "treated" and reeducated in the doctrines of Communism, and genetically screened for selective breeding, or singled out as candidates for possible cloning.

SUBLIMINAL CONDITIONING

The research into subliminal technology is continuing, and is too highly classified and complex to discuss in detail, within the general scope of Psychopolitics. Suffice it to say that a similar phenomenon which operates on the conscious level, and whose effect is directly observable as immediate cause/effect is the adverse influence which "Rap" or "hip-hop" music (the term "music" is used loosely here) has on the listener. With its repetitive 3-note background mantras, and endless strings of incoherent, meaningless, psychotic expletives and *non-sequiturs*, this is brainwashing at its very best using "talent" at its utmost worst.

Upon experimentation, you will find that "Rap" and "hip-hop" music, are mediums uniquely suited for the purpose of disrupting the "law and order" of any society, provided the subjects can be conditioned to tolerate and then enjoy listening to it. "Rap" music was used to get Manuel Noriega, the infamous Drug
Lord, to evacuate his bunker and walk into the waiting arms of InterPol.[218]

As a rule every Darwinist knows, the more feeble-minded or less evolved a person's brain is, the more tolerant of abuse a person, or race, is. This speaks volumes of the people whose "culture" revolves around this type of "music". These Neanderthals are not exactly what one would be looking for if one were selecting candidates for Neo-

---

[218] InterPol – an international police organization.

Eugenics; however each segment of the society – even these dregs, can be put to use to achieve Party objectives, if psychopoliticians take care to be ingenious and inventive.

HELTER-SKELTER

In ages past, within a totalitarian society, the inferior races were marked for elimination, and then systematically disposed of, such as the Jews in World War II, and numerous other examples. Modern Psychopolitics has abandoned the promotion of outright genocide, in favor of the skillful manipulation of undesirables and those who are genetically inferior or mentally deficient; those who are insufficiently evolved, and infidels to the cause; to use them as an instrument to inflict social chaos. The target of that directed chaos would be that segment of the society we seek to control.

By the constant infliction of social unrest, random, senseless, and brutal acts of violence and escalating paranoia inflicted by the "undesirables" under or covert control, the desirable portion of the masses will seek the protection of the Communist State.

Of course, once the desirable segment of the population; the purebred, the educated, the professionals, and the cream of the working class, the well-evolved and genetically superior have surrendered their freedom to the Party in exchange for the Party's "protective custody", the State can then eliminate the inferiors in a legally contrived civil unrest put-down, executing them with the full sanction of the politically captive intelligentsia. We will then have achieved our long-awaited and earnestly sought-after Leninist Utopia without firing a shot.

IN CONCLUSION

The long battle, fought on the ideological frontier, is now nearly over. We stand just a few short steps, and a very short distance from the pinnacle of a complete victory. We must take extreme caution not to awaken the Samson[219] "America", until we have thoroughly entangled his hair in the weaver's shuttle.[220]

If I may be permitted to construct a fitting paraphrase of a verse from the Christian's Bible:

"...The weapons of the psychopolitician are not carnal, but mighty through psychology to the pulling down of Imperialist-Capitalist strong-holds; casting down imaginations and every high ideal that exalts itself above the wisdom of the Party and the authority of the State, and bringing into submission every thought, to the obedience of Lenin and Marx."   - 2nd Corinthians 10:4, 5 - paraphrased

With this fitting quotation taken from "the opiate of the masses", I bid my comrades farewell, and *Nostrovia!* [221] And to our brothers in Berlin, *Zieg Heil!* [222]

"PEACE"

Shurhaff Kummalongvay[223]

---

[219] See: Judges 13:24 to 16:30
[220] See: Judges 16:13-14
[221] "Nostrovia" – a Russian toast (with drinks).
[222] "Zeig Heil" – the Nazi salute given to Adolph Hitler during WWII.
[223] "Shurhaff Kummalongvay" – a fictitious name to sound like: "Sure have come a long way".

PLANS FOR THE FUTURE

An addendum to:
A synthesis of the Russian Textbook on Psychopolitics
© Copyright 2004 - David Todeschini - all rights reserved

INTRODUCTION

By: Ayeville Kutchakokkov[224]

As the well taught student of Psychopolitics knows, in order to be successful in psychological warfare, the attack must proceed on as many vectors as possible. This is an extremely effective tactic because it introduces what has come to be known in the field of black Dianetics as "wide-field randomity" into the enemy's society. In layman's terms, so many things are going wrong, that the enemy under attack cannot find a single stable reference point from which to calculate a possible defense. With wide field randomity, each instance of cause and effect becomes increasingly nebulous as more elements of randomity are added. This leads to the phenomenon that creates the apparency of each call is being uncaused, and every effect being its own cause. The student can observe the results of this by noticing the endless debates about *"Do violent movies and TV programs cause violence, or do people with violent personalities naturally seek violence in their entertainment?"* Do guns cause people to shoot people, or do people who want to kill somebody go looking for a gun to do it with?" In a society that is severely randomized via the covert ops of Party operatives, the answer to both those questions is simply, *"Yes".*

No adversary in military history has ever been able to defend an attack by multiple forces allied against him, and operating independently but simultaneously. If the defender focuses his effort along any one vector he must of necessity, sacrifice attention and

---

[224] Ayeville Kutchakokkov is a fictitious name – David Todeschini is writing this "in his stead".

efforts to defend or counterattack along all the remaining ones. His eventual defeat is a *fait accompli.*

Psyops has long recognized that the most effective means by which to induce wide-field randomity into any society, is to remove (or randomly move) the society's moral anchors or points-of-reference. The Prime "moral anchor" of American society: The foundation, upon which the Republic was built, was the immutable and static (unchanging) moral code of Judeo-Christian, Biblical absolutes. Upon this, the U.S. Constitution was drafted with the full intent of the founders, to stand as the codification of an inviolable covenant agreement between the group governed, and the governed members of the government. Anchored solidly in what was agreed to be Divine law, the nation was intended to be, and to remain forever, a Christian Constitutional Republic.

The Party had, since the early 1950s, recognized that the single most stabilizing factor in American culture and society was the near-universal belief in God - not just any God, but the God of Judeo-Christianity. Upon tracing America's strength back to its source, the Party embarked upon a well-contrived plan to subvert and subduct the Judeo-Christian underpinnings of the nation called the United States. A bit of history, albeit superficially covered here, when the Party's perspective, will serve to crystallize the students point of view into the future, and solidify his confidence not only in the Party's goals and objectives, but also in the time-tested psychopolitical tactics taught at Lenin University.

Party efforts to collapse the American government began in earnest in the early 1900s with the institution of a graduated Federal income tax, the contrived economic depression, and the institution of Social Security. The pivotal battles in this war of ideologies in the past 50 years are well-documented history, but their true underlying causes have never been suspected.

The Neo-Nexus of the current decadence of the society can be statistically traced back to 1963, when the mention of God was removed from the public schools by court decree. Hinging upon this political victory, every statistical assessment of societal progress and stability immediately nose-dived. Knowing precisely what was going to happen, Party operatives and dupes, psychiatrists and psychologists infiltrated schools and government institutions, and have since been instrumental in causing still more areas of randomity, chaos, and intractable spiritual confusion.

With the Biblical anchor of moral absolutes effectively neutralized, the entire "field" of cognitive ethical computations came unglued. It was therefore child's play for psychopolitical agents and dupes to introduce Darwinian evolution into the textbooks, as the "scientific" argument against the Biblical Creation account, the refutation of God and against the lofty, outdated, and "old-fashioned" rules of behavior.

Ten years later, the psychopolitical organization *Planned Parenthood* was waiting in the wings to support the idea that a baby *in vivo* is not really a human being yet. Thus the decision in Roe v. Wade[225] came about in order that unwed mothers, primarily Negroes, Hispanics, and other less-evolved races, could have the sanction of law, and the financial support of the government to terminate their pregnancies. As a collateral benefit, they could absolve themselves from the consequences of their animal instinct to mate. The government is all too-willing to "invest" $300 to pay for the abortion of a child that would, if not aborted, likely have to be maintained by law on the public dole for the rest of his or her natural life. From the standpoint of an impersonal and cold government bureaucracy, it is an equitable trade.

---

[225] Roe v. Wade, 410 US 113, S. Ct. 705 (1973)

Lest the Party become so full of itself that we boast of our "ingenuity" in the purposeful engineering of chaos and randomity that was not even foreseen, much-less planned, suffice it to say honestly; many of these Domino-effect events had not been in the original PsyOps plan or forecast. However, what we can say with a certainty is a quote of an axiom of physics: "order or structure cannot arise from randomity"; it is the second law of thermodynamics. In the Lehman's vernacular, it is perhaps easier to explain and comprehend this principle, using an analogy:

American society, like any civilized society, is an extremely complex machine with a litany of moving, interacting, and interdependent parts - not unlike gears, and levers, motors, springs, ratchets and escapements in a large industrial machine. A Party cooperative or psychopolitician is the "Dutchman saboteur (the word 'sabotage' originated in Holland, where Dutch workers destroyed machines by throwing their wooden shoes - sabots - into the gears) standing on a catwalk overlooking the mechanism, monkey-wrench in hand. The only "plan" in the mind of the Dutchman is whatever cognitive process that causes him to stand at the rail, and upon observing the mechanism in action, the reasoning process that leads to a decision as to which part of the machine that is accessible to him, is most vulnerable to the introduction of a monkey wrench. The psychopolitician or Party agent, like the Dutchman, cannot possibly foresee the precise effect of the act of throwing that wrench into the "works"; all he knows is that the mechanism surely won't work any better for his having thrown a wrench into the gears.

And so, a psychopolitician, while he can know with precision the effect of his *sabot* thrown into the workings of Imperialist-Capitalist society, he cannot possibly predict the cascade of events that inevitably follow. Many times, the collateral damage unintended and unplanned, is more exquisitely wonderful than the initial "clunk" of the gears as the machine "ate" that wrench. The end-result of sabotage is chaos, and an expenditure of both manpower and money in an attempt to repair the damage.

The truly astute operative who is always distinguished and esteemed above his peers, plans his operations carefully. When "the shit hits the fan", as they say, he will be in a position to play the part of the hero; the Knight in shining armor that comes to the rescue; the arsonist with a book of matches in one hand, and fire extinguisher in the other. *When the barn is burning, nobody asks you if you are a fireman; if you happen to be holding a hose, they'll pay you to use it. Nobody will suspect that you set the fire, if you're standing there trying to put it out.* The most difficult part of being a psychopolitician is learning how to switch valences quickly, and being confident enough in your methodology to appear credible in the role of the hero or savior, when you are actually the "villain" who created the problem or incited the trouble.

It is a true datum, and worthy to be committed to memory, that: In order to believe a lie, one has to first, stop believing the truth; and once one stops believing the truth, it is then possible to make a person believe anything. The psychopolitician, being trained to assume many different valences or identities in order to be convincing and appear genuine, runs the inevitable risk of "playing the part" so well, **it is possible that he will come to believe his own bullshit.** And in this condition, an operative who has accomplished a task for the Party, cannot be reassigned unless he can first be debriefed. In a majority of cases, PsyOps has found that **advanced stages of this condition are intractable**. The "up-side" of this condition is that should be operative be discovered and questioned by authorities, he could pass a polygraph test and interrogation on the Sodium Pentothal[226] with flying colors. There is no question at this point, that Socialism will prevail if current trends continue, and our methods remain cloaked in the veil of credibility that PsyOps has so skillfully contrived.

---

[226] Sodium Pentothal – otherwise known as "Truth Serum".

THE PASSION OF THE CHRIST

Dear comrades, do not be discouraged by what will appear at first, to be major setbacks, but in reality, are merely "flashes in the pan". FieldOps and PsyOps have been swamped with e-mails and crypto-coms[227] from field agents more troubled about the massive public response to Mel Gibson's film "The Passion of the Christ". Reliable reports claimed that *"hardened unbelievers came out of the theaters weeping uncontrollably; many gave their hearts to Christ"*. Well? I ask you comrades, so what? Even a drone of the State is entitled to a bit of good entertainment, is he not? The Passion is a very moving story; but it's just a story. Brilliantly portrayed, yes, absolutely! Give the man (Mel Gibson) credit for credit is certainly due, but recognize the story for what it is. It will pass.

By no means, however strongly you may feel about it, should you attack anyone's religious convictions directly. To do so, will only drive them into that condition of "asserted rightness" covered previously, and that very mechanism, codified by our late nemesis L. Ron Hubbard; that precise mechanism that psychologists and legislators so skillfully employ to create incorrigible criminals, works equally well, if provoked, to create die-hard Christians! Be mindful, comrades that the major component of confusion in "wide-field randomity" is the "background" or the reliable reference point by which to relative motion of all the other viewpoints can be perceived or cognitively discerned. If the anchor point can be reestablished, a very great amount of absolutely brilliant and deviously cunning work, millions of man-hours and countless trillions of Rubles invested in The Master Plan, will have been for naught.

We seek evolution from a God-centered Constitutional Republic with immutable moral absolutes, to government (man) centered Democracy with floating and drifting independent "free

---

[227] "Crypto-coms" – encrypted messages or communications.

agent" moral philosophers. We strive to establish a Socialist State where the masses are ruled by the Illuminati – and this can only come about gradually, just as the species Homo Sapiens Sapiens gradually arose out of the primordial slime. We cannot afford to attempt to force a "punctuated equilibrium" upon a natural evolutionary process.

FIELD RANDOMITY

The concept of field randomity is essential to the Psychopolitician's ability to function effectively towards achieving the goals of the Party. In figure A, the "ship" of morality, ethics, and Justice is tied closely to an immutable moral standard[228] ("anchor"). All other events (represented by the ovals) are judged relative to the static absolute. With a stable anchor point, the motions of all the other variables can be accurately discerned. In figure B, the ship is loosely bound to an unstable, changing, and unpredictable, and unreliable point of reference.[229] In this case, truth is a matter of opinion and right and wrong cannot be adjudicated. Other events cannot be reliably judged, as all elements are in random motion, even the "anchor".

To be able to introduce maximum chaos into a society, and to therefore be the sought-after "savior", the astute psychopolitician strives to keep ethical and moral absolutes out of the enemy's society.

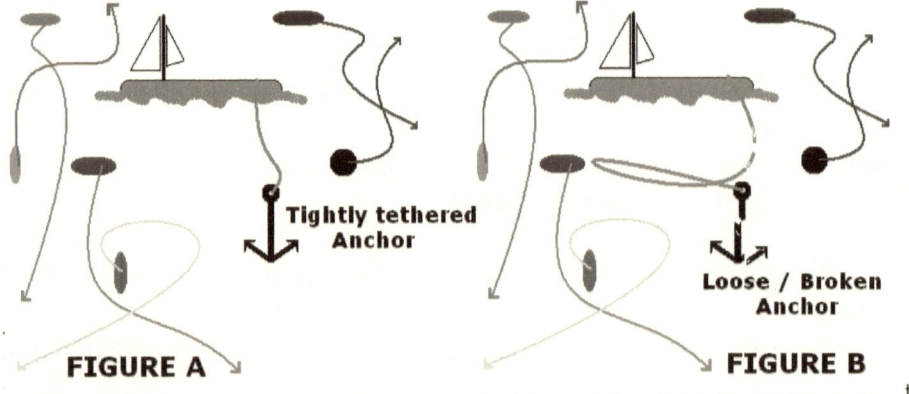

FIGURE A   Tightly tethered Anchor

FIGURE B   Loose / Broken Anchor

the idea that each person becomes his or her own "moral philosopher" that is the unstable point-of-reference.

THE "WORLD COURT"

In order for One World Government to work, there has to be a system of judicial review which can supersede and override the decisions of the US Supreme Court, and the national courts of all other sovereign nations. The Hague is the predecessor to this world court; the military UN forces will enforce its decisions. At present, Mexico is petitioning the World Court to "order the US to retry 52 Mexicans on death row was here because they weren't told of their right to consular help. 55 Mexicans with such aid avoided the death penalty".[230]

PsyOps is primarily responsible for creating the public demand to try children in adult courts for certain crimes. Politicians have capitulated to their demands, and as a result, many preadolescents have been executed. In classic "Wolf in sheep's clothing" style, these masters of psychobabble, using the compassion of the public for the young children executed under their hue and cry, are attempting to have the World Court outlaw the execution of juveniles.

While the protection of children is a noble cause; and the lesser culpability or *mens rea*[231] of a young child is recognized even by Third World Banana Republics, the US still imposes the death penalty on children - the children that had committed crimes under the influence of experimental psychotropic drugs given to them against their will, to treat them for fictitious diseases that the Merchants of Chaos themselves, invented.

If World Court is successful in banning child executions, it will convince the American people that their courts were wrong to allow a child to be murdered by the State. (The courts are wrong by any rational impetus, to sentence a 12-year-old to death). This is all by

---

[230] Source: Justicia newsletter, Jan-Feb '04 - ISSN1077-6516 page 11, ¶2
[231] *"Mens rea"* - (Latin, legal term) - "a guilty mind".

design, in order to "light the fire" so that the Party becomes the heroes, when we show up, fire-hose in hand.

The situation is complex, and is the result of unforeseen collateral damage which is in turn, caused by wide field randomity caused by the patriotic sabot thrown into the "gears" of public education by our operatives in the field. And, as is the case with all collateral chaos, it provides future "Dutchman saboteurs" the opportunity to assume the valence of a firefighter, hose in hand, awaiting an opportune moment to dump gasoline onto the Inferno. Randomity and chaos always works to the Party's advantage, especially when we can cause Socialism to appear as a fixed point (static) in a field where everything else is in random motion.

A Nation into which extreme levels of chaos can be introduced, will quickly sink into a state of apathy. This is because decisions based on false or random data, or made from unstable viewpoints - such as moral relativism or "New Age" post-modernism - yield results or effects which are equally as unpredictable as the data from which analytical minds calculate solutions. When any decision within the realm of postulated choices (based on the data available) results in an undesirable outcome, the organism quickly computes that "I can't win", and thereafter avoids making decisions. The function of psychopolitician is to create chaos, so that - to paraphrase a part of the Christians Bible:

"...They are again the entangled therein, and overcome, the latter end is worse with them than the beginning". - 2 Peter 2:20b (KJV)

The "solution" to them, is to turn to the fireman with a hose. When it is perceived that relying on Socialism produces a predictable (not necessarily desirable) result, the masses will opt for Socialism, because it is well documented by our late nemesis of Dianetics fame, that man seeks to "play the game" by becoming cause over effect…it really is of secondary consequence what that effect might be. Being "cause over effect", in other words, having control – or the apparency of control – is better than having NO control. It is the function of the psychopolitician to create that apparency, and cause the general population to accept the apparency as "real".

ENEMY TECH

It is certainly true that any beneficial technology that has ever been developed can be used to harm. Conversely, any harmful technology that has ever been developed can be directed toward benevolent. For example, the same tech developed to wipe out Hiroshima and Nagasaki is now used to generate electricity. Antibiotics and DNA technology, developed to cure disease, has been used to create very own strains of bacteria, and to engineer viruses for biological weapons.

On the same level, Dianetics, which is the only efficable technology for resolving trauma-based problems, can be 'flipped', and used to inflict mental problems. Understanding the mechanism of the human mind is the key to being able to manipulate a single person, or an entire population. KGB/PsyOps currently uses what L. Ron Hubbard himself called "Black Dianetics", after realizing that the science he developed was indeed a two-edged sword.

However, any serious student of Socialism knows that the founding fathers Lenin and Marx had been using "psychology" to further the cause of Socialism long before Dianetics. All that "Black Dianetics" does for the psychopolitician, is to clarify the understanding put forth by Dianetics in order to codify methods by which a person or society may be influenced with predictable results; it is a much more efficient methodology than the former blind brutality. In fact, the use of

Black Dianetics techniques are revolutionizing the infliction of brutality… it is like removing a gallbladder with a grappling hook through the urethra; it hurts like hell, but requires no sutures - no visible evidence of the operation. The patient is "minus" a gallbladder, and nobody believes how it was done.

ORWELLIAN LINGUISTICS

"NewSpeak" - the coined word that sci-fi author George Orwell used to describe "A rose by any other name" is really nothing new. Actually, the nomenclature *sub nom* reaches far back into antiquity.

In more modern times, just prior to the appearance of Orwell's novel of the international fame "1984", the usefulness of calling something undesirable or repulsive by another name, was recognized and codified into "routine" PsyOps procedures. Its close cousin is "Political Correctness".

Within the last 20 years or so, New Speak has evolved into two separate and distinct "animals". The first is the familiar "Political Correctness", and the other, not commonly known "definition inversion". In the latter the meaning of the word and its opposite word (antecedent) is not as defined in the dictionary, but "swapped" in usage and in practice. A good example is the word "tolerance".

In the dictionary, tolerance is defined as forbearance and long-suffering (patience) with something that is NOT liked or DISAGREEABLE for the sake of respect of another person. In American society today, if you tolerate something, it means that you agree with it. If you do not agree, according to this line of reasoning, it follows that you are being intolerant. And so it is that tolerance becomes intolerance, and disagreeing with a point of view, an opinion, a law, or lifestyle that is repulsive to you, gets you called "intolerant" by the opposition.

This brilliant piece of social engineering by the party's psycholinguistics division of PsyOps, gets a person who thinks abortion is murder, labeled as intolerant of "choice". "Choice" is the sanitized name for infanticide; a gets a person who has a Biblical view of human sexuality - someone in whose eyes homosexuality is "an abomination unto the Lord" labeled as intolerant of " gays" - the *sub nom* sanitation of " sodomite". There are hundreds of examples.

This phenomenon is such a marvelous collateral effect of the "dumbed-down" education system, if the Party could codify how it could be engineered, a claim could be made that we engineered it. However "definition inversion" evolved out of stupidity, and there can be no accounting for the effects of the pursuit of ignorance.

PsyOps/Psycholinguistics experts unanimously agree that this collateral effect could not be any more suited to the purpose of disrupting the accuracy of communication had it been purposefully engineered. One researcher commented to this author:

"We've been studying this phenomenon for the past 15 years or so, and we can't get away from the temptation to conclude that some unknown psycholinguistics lab somewhere, engineered this thing.... it's that radical! We also had many brainstorming sessions trying to figure out how to reverse engineer this thing into a language. We concluded after many thousands of man-hours of looking into German, French, Spanish, Italian, and Norwegian languages, that definition inversion is unique to the English language; it is a vulnerability that is built into the language structure. It is impossible to contrive any semblance of this mechanism into Hebrew, Greek, or Aramaic. This phenomenon has us completely at a loss for an explanation. Fate has it that it happens to work to our advantage. The enemy's communication is becoming so twisted and aberrated by this phenomenon, that in a 20 years, or so, Americans will be using sign language or drawings pictures on paper napkins to order a cup of coffee in a diner".

We must point out here, to avoid potential confusion, that definition inversion is not "slang", or any "ghetto tongue" nor does it appear to have arisen out of those anomalies. Although it is the result of psycholinguistics and "Outcome-based Education", it is completely uncontrived. It appears to be primarily the result of the incompetence of the school curriculum - specifically, in the almost total failure of the new age educational methodology to define the words as they are used, encountered, or taught. The proof of this conclusion is that experiments with young adults known to be afflicted with this aberration, are no longer so affected after Dianetics Word Clearing™ [232] is done.

GLOBAL HUMAN GENOME PROJECT / DNA DATABASE

The Kremlin has covertly purchased (through third and fourth parties), 12 fluorine cooled Cray YM/PC -120 supercomputers each capable of 120 billion FPS (FLOating-Point operations per Second) - or in the technical vernacular "120 giga flops", P-7 processors, and 2000 trillion gigabytes of wide SCSI hard disks. This equipment is being used exclusively to store DNA information, and to perform statistical analysis on the available database, to determine if certain nonphysical traits such as intelligence, criminality, stubbornness, apathy, persistence, and a variety of talents are predispositions or are coded in DNA, or if they can be " passed on" genetically or engineered in the laboratory. The KGB has acquired access to the FBI's DNA database via embedded double agents, and research is being conducted under unprecedented security measures. Further research, it is hoped that Bio-Ops can draw the information to enable the engineering of "target-

---

[232] Word Clearing is the process of defining a word as soon as a misunderstood or unknown word is encountered. This is the reason for the effusive footnotes here. By "Word Clearing" what you read, your comprehension and vocabulary skills soar.

specific" viruses, potentially targetable[233] to a single race, or even specific to a single individual, in theory.

SELECTIVE BIOTOXINS

Without embarking on a necessarily lengthy tome on biology, suffice it to say that the DNA technology is relatively new, and in fact, in its infancy. There is no telling what the future will bring, but for the sake of argument, let us postulate that just five years from now, our boys in biotech can engineer a retrovirus that is DNA specific; that is, it remains harmless in the absence of a DNA molecule that has a specific genome sequence in it. With such a capability, while weapons could be produced, which target only the races are "nationalities" or types of individuals selected. Developed to this point (which is theoretically possible), and further refined to the next logical step, it may be possible, given a sample of DNA to work from (a strand of hair, or a nail clipping), to design a retrovirus specific to a single individual in a high-tech genetics lab.

Possession of this technology will enable us to eliminate any opposition at will. A president, a political nemesis, an infidel - anyone - could be targeted by either saturating his environment with the biotoxins overtly (such as introducing the pathogen into a buildings air-conditioning system), or by infecting those who come in contact with him (reporters at a news conference). The carriers or vectors would remain unaffected. The "target" will then appear to have died of "natural causes". The autopsy would find no presence of any known pathogen. The "engineered" virus will have caused no illnesses or deaths elsewhere; CDC would not even be able to detect it, or even if it was isolated, could not, without the technology, know that it was designed, or what it was designed to do.

---

[233] "Targetable" – able to be targeted.

COVERTLY; IN THE DARK; BEHIND THE SCENES; ABOVE SUSPICION

Even those phrases should be the Psychopolitician's mantra and meditation, as he goes forth among the Imperialist Capitalist Dogs, awaiting the opportunity to sow the seeds of turmoil, and to hurl his sabot into the Leviathan machine. Those ideals faithfully followed, is the legacy of Party pioneers: we should not have come this far without them. It would indeed be foolish to abandon what has served the cause so well.

There are those that will try to convince you not to be so bold in the carrying out of your mission; they will tell you - or you may be tempted to convince yourself - that "audacity increases the risk of discovery". This might seem logical but it is not true. Outrageousness, committed in the valence of the fireman with his hose at-the-ready, is never discovered. And if it is suspected, it is most efficiently dealt with by more outrageousness. In the immortal words of Robespierre during the French Revolution: *"Audacity, audacity; always audacity!"*. His downfall came when he ran out audacity, and he allowed himself to be made into a joke - a laughingstock. An old woman in her dementia, confessed him as a god, and said that she, being pregnant by him, would give birth to the French Messiah. Read your history. The people, who formerly feared him, now laughed him to scorn. His grip on the nation was broken because laughter overcomes fear, and in the absence of fear, men can discern the truth. Because of his inability or his reluctance to become more audacious, he eventually lost his head - literally! (Read *"Robespierre - The Voice of Virtue"* - by Otto Scott).

There are lessons to be learned from history; studying the rise and fall of great leaders. I will charge the student of psychopolitics to take great pains to learn the lessons well.

It may seem to some people who read this, that flagrant audacity and covertness - a "hidden agenda", if you will, are non-sequiturs, or oxymorons. This is not so. All one has to do to convince himself that it is not so, is to observe the sequence of events when a bright exuberant child is consigned to the care and trust of a merchant of chaos:

The child is bored for lack of stimulation at his intellectual level.
He fights and can't "pay attention" - he is bored and craves action and attention.
Sent to a "therapist", he is diagnosed with a AHDD and medicated.
The drugs "cure" his restlessness – The physical "jitters" becomes suppressed mental agitation.
Perceptions are warped by the drugs; paranoia leads to covert hostility.
Suppressed hostility erupts into physical violence unpredictably.
He is "treated" by counseling that keeps an "in valence".
His "meditation" is increased; inhibitions fall away.
What is left of his cognitive ability asserts the "rightness" of his behavior by repeating it, and becoming more violent.
He falls into the hands of the law, prison, and it finishes him.

The audacity exists at step number three when the child is given drugs to treat a nonexistent totally fictitious disorder. When the effect of the drugs and equally audacious "treatment" (step seven) cause more problems, "always audacity" steps in, and gives you more of what not only doesn't work, but what caused the problem to start with (step eight). The culprits - drugs and psychiatry - are never discovered. They are not even suspected, because we made a public believe that normal, youthful exuberance is a "disorder", the most that will be charged to the "fault" or the "shortcomings" of child psychology is that it cannot "cure" hyperactivity. Of course, this is preferable to the charge that "HDD does not exist", because we are the experts, and we say "It does exist", and how is the opposition going to prove otherwise, while the society-at-large, and the courts, hold psychiatry and psychology in such high regard?

If you want an example of how this quackery is worshiped as a deity, all you have to do is look at a psychiatrist's income. People will pay thousands of dollars to be counseled about their grief over a dead cat, and be "in therapy" for years. ***True story***: one of our civilian *cum laude* graduates recently found a well-to-do patient, and diagnosed her with "multiple personality disorder". Among the many valences he "discovered" (but could not "run out") was **a duck that talked to God. (Talk about a quack!)**. *"Audacity, audacity, always audacity!"*. Had Robespierre the benefit of the training here at London University, he would've had the audacity and the credibility to make the French people believe without question, that old woman's claim. She could have been the Biblical Sarah, and he could have been Abraham. Instead of going to the guillotine, he and his elderly concubine could've had a glorious end! His agenda was hidden; he operated covertly; he was above suspicion and beyond reproach. He was "The Voice of Virtue", until audacity came up short.

BRIEFLY – IN CLOSING

My dear comrades, you here at Lenin University, are fortunate to be educated in the greatest time, and in the most prestigious school in man's history. You will learn to abandon conscience, study deception, and cultivate cunning. You will be fearless, and bold, and confident, because what you will be taught has been thoroughly tested and proven to work and work infallibly. Our growth lies in the effectiveness of what has been done thus far. And in that knowledge you can be comfortable in a sea of audacity and you will triumph in your attainment of Party objectives. Our utopia will be won... It is ours!

A Synthesis of The Russian Brainwashing Manual on Psychopolitics

Bookstore: www.LuLu.com/Net4TruthUSA

Land of Childhood's Fears - Faith, Friendship, and The Vietnam War
http://www.LuLu.com/content/210444   ISBN 1-4116-2452-1 Paperback - ISBN # 1-4116-7111-2 - Hardcover

The Lie Detection Manual - Become a Human Lie Detector - Never be lied to again.
http://www.LuLu.com/content/88212   ISBN 1-4116-1821-1

Entertaining Angels - Bible Bedtime Stories, poetry, and humorous stories for Children.
http://www.LuLu.com/content/104158

A Book of Sermons vol 1 and 2 - Sermons from WebPastor Dave's awesome web site.
http://www.LuLu.com/content/213421

Psychiatry and Confession - a reprint of a 1948 publication of the Catholic Church w/commentary.
http://www.LuLu.com/content/87831.

The Sexual Paraphilias - Therapy by Hick-Farmer Sigmund Freud Wannabes - Psychiatry in America.
http://www.LuLu.com/content/91782

The Battered Spouse and The Abused Child - A pastoral analysis of domestic violence.
http://www.LuLu.com/content/88267.

Please Don't Do This - A book for women contemplating an abortion (pro life).
http://www.LuLu.com/content/89914

The Book of NeoGenesis The evolution of Man from rocks - a spoof on the Darwinist Pagam religion.
http://www.LuLu.com/content/89015

Psychiatry, Mind Control, Genocide and Infanticide - Psychiatry is the root of all wars since WWI.
http://www.LuLu.com/content/92111

Net4TruthUSA - NEWSLETTERS - HTML and PDF versions available
Go to www.Net4TruthUSA.com/newsletters.htm

CATALOG OF PRODUCTS - FREE FOR DOWNLOADING
An updated product catalog can be found at: http://www.LuLu.com/content/92031.

www.ingramcontent.com/pod-product-compliance
Lightning Source LLC
Chambersburg PA
CBHW020441290526
45785CB00002B/956